Classroom Dilemmas

Classroom Dilemmas

Solutions for Everyday Problems

Richard B. Kimbrough

ROWMAN & LITTLEFIELD
Lanham • Boulder • New York • London

Published by Rowman & Littlefield
A wholly owned subsidiary of The Rowman & Littlefield Publishing Group, Inc.
4501 Forbes Boulevard, Suite 200, Lanham, Maryland 20706
www.rowman.com

Unit A, Whitacre Mews, 26-34 Stannary Street, London SE11 4AB

Copyright © 2015 by Richard B. Kimbrough

All rights reserved. No part of this book may be reproduced in any form or by any electronic or mechanical means, including information storage and retrieval systems, without written permission from the publisher, except by a reviewer who may quote passages in a review.

British Library Cataloguing in Publication Information Available

Library of Congress Cataloging-in-Publication Data

Kimbrough, Richard B., 1931–
Classroom dilemmas : solutions for everyday problems / Richard B. Kimbrough.
pages cm
ISBN 978-1-4758-2058-4 (cloth : alk. paper) — ISBN 978-1-4758-2059-1 (pbk. : alk. paper) — ISBN 978-1-4758-2060-7 (electronic)
1. Classroom management. I. Title.
LB3013.K566 2015
371.102'4—dc23
2015013181

∞ ™ The paper used in this publication meets the minimum requirements of American National Standard for Information Sciences Permanence of Paper for Printed Library Materials, ANSI/NISO Z39.48-1992.

Printed in the United States of America

Contents

Preface		vii
Introduction		ix
1	Lesson Plans: Orders or Suggestions	1
2	Arturo's Eligibility	5
3	History Taught "Backward"	11
4	Homework—Yes or No	15
5	Cullen's Grade?	19
6	Bernie's Grade?	23
7	The Trumpet Thief	27
8	Charley's Boy	31
9	A Jihadist in the School	35
10	Mr. Martin's Titles	39
11	To Run? Not to Run?	43
12	The Absentees	47
13	Patty v. the Bully	51
14	Love in the Classroom	55
15	Santa or Satan	59
16	No News Is Good News	63
17	Poaching for Profit	67
18	Religion, Racism, and Rumor	71
19	The Power of Money	77
20	Buffaloes and Free Throws	81
21	Snake!!!	85
22	Making the Tackle	89
23	Genius in the Classroom	93
24	The Hunter	97
25	The Paddler	101
26	The Precious Lost Ball	105
27	The Banned Wife	109

28	The Dog in the Classroom	113
29	The Boy with ESP	117
30	A Trip to the Dentist	121
31	Climate Change	125
32	Boy or Girl?	129
33	Baggy Pants	133
34	Up the Down Stairs	137
35	Here Come Better Grades	141
36	Precious	145
About the Author		147

Preface

As a teacher and principal for fifty-seven years I have seen or heard about all manner of interesting behaviors in the field of education, some highly inspirational, some appallingly disgusting, ranging from the very serious to the capricious to the hilarious.

In this book I seek to illustrate one prominent educational issue and to foster discussion on that issue, namely the handling of educational dilemmas. Educators at every level regularly face dilemmas regarding how to deal with particular situations arising around the question: "In this situation do I do what I think best for the student, teacher, school, or other person or entity involved, or do I abide by school policy which may or may not be best?"

Most of the dilemmas discussed here are quite common in one form or another. Nearly every educator has dealt with a similar situation if he or she has been in the education field for any length of time.

For example, in the second dilemma presented here, is it better to permit Arturo to participate in the one school activity at which he excels, even though his grades make him ineligible, or will letting him participate corrode and corrupt the school's entire eligibility policy? Every principal, dean, or coach has dealt with this dilemma or one quite similar.

Another example: in the third story should Sunny be dismissed because she persists in teaching American history "backward," contrary to the chronological method used by the other history teachers in the school, or should Sunny be permitted to teach in the style she finds most beneficial to and enjoyable for her students?

While I have changed the names of the educators and students involved as well as the schools in which the dilemmas occurred, be assured that each did occur and much in the manner I describe.

At the end of each story I have provided evidence and opinion to support a decision on either side of the dilemma. "Pro" will take one side of the matter. "Con" will take the other side.

And finally, the resolution to the matter as it actually was resolved is presented.

As a school administrator, teacher, coach, parent, or student, you may ask yourself which side would you have supported—and why?

Introduction

Each chapter in *Classroom Dilemmas* is composed of five parts.

The situation with which the educator(s) (teacher, administrator, board of education) must deal is set out first. This is a problem akin to problems faced regularly by persons in the business of educating K–12 students.

The second part of each chapter spells out the dilemma faced by the educator charged with making a decision relating to the problem. While the way to solve the problem may be clear to one person, the opposite way is equally obvious to another, and to a third person—most persons— the situation defies neat resolution; i.e., it creates a dilemma. The decision maker must choose between two alternatives—or sometimes more—and each alternative presents both positive and negative aspects; i. e., "If I do this, that might be the result, but if I do that, this might be the result."

The third part of the chapter is the "Pro" argument in which one or the other of the possible decisions is defended, citing facts and opinions to support his/her argument. It is important to recognize that not *all* of the possible reasons to embrace this or that decision are given. These are only some of the typical arguments given. Certainly a number of other, and sometimes more relevant and substantial, arguments might be presented.

In the fourth part of the chapter the "Con" argument is presented in which one or the other of the possible decisions is attacked, the attack being in the same form as the defense; i.e., opinions, facts, but not *all* relevant opinions and/or facts.

While both the "Pro" and the "Con" sides do make mostly valid arguments, both also make some assertions that are false.

The fifth part of the chapter tells how the dilemma was actually resolved. Occasionally the resolution is Solomon-like in that every one or almost every one of those affected by the decision are pleased with the decision—or can at least tolerate it. More often, however, depending on how the dilemma was resolved, supporters of either the "Pro" side or the "Con" side are displeased to a greater or lesser degree.

Each chapter is organized in this way to best present the types of dilemmas that educators face and thus the tough and many times unpopular decisions they must make.

The reader is permitted and encouraged to decide what his/her decision would have been had he/she faced the same dilemma.

ONE
Lesson Plans: Orders or Suggestions

After retiring from teaching English for forty-two years in a small Midwestern high school, Walter Parker moved to a city of more than two hundred thousand with five public high schools. There he answered the call for substitute teachers. His first assignment was to substitute for an English teacher in an inner-city high school.

Upon arriving at the school Parker learned he was to substitute for a Ms. Fellows, a first-year teacher. Parker went to her room and read the lesson plan for his first class, a class in world literature. Ms. Fellows wanted the students to read a short story and then write answers to questions from their textbooks relating to the story.

Before the students arrived in the classroom Parker previewed the story. He had never heard of the author, and he found the story quite pedestrian and unappealing. But he had been given the lesson plan, and he intended to follow it.

Presently the students trooped in. When they learned their assignment they rebelled immediately, voicing strong objections to what they were to do.

While Parker quite agreed with the students' assessment of the story as having little relevance in their lives he was not yet ready to say so aloud. Instead, in a cool, quiet voice, he said, "You know, I've always thought world literature quite interesting. Some stories are more interesting than others, of course, but . . ."

The students interrupted to state their contrary opinion, one saying, "None of this junk is interesting. It's all just junk." The others agreed en masse.

Right then Parker made a decision. Because he could not bear the thought of students completing their youth and probably their entire lives thinking a subject he loved, world literature, was "junk," he decided to jettison Ms. Fellows's lesson plan in an effort to change the students' minds about world literature.

Parker began by saying, "World literature means just that. It comes from all over the world so we can learn about other cultures. What we learn most is how similar people are, how we all have the same basic drives and desires, some good, some bad. Let me tell you two or three stories. You'll see what I mean."

He then told three stories, one from the Russian author Tolstoy, a second from the Englishman Saki, and the third from the American Eudora Welty. In turn the stories told of the sin of greed, the importance of friendships, and the need to persist.

At the end of his third story Parker asked if the students had comments or questions. Yes, indeed they did, all manner of comments and questions, some generating considerable passion; e.g., when does a desire for acquisition become greed? Why are people greedy? Is death all we really have to look forward to? Why do people hate each other? What is true friendship? Does Welty's story symbolically represent the plight of African Americans living in the United States after the abolition of slavery?

When the buzzer ended the period, the students actually rose and cheered. Several asked when Parker would return to their classroom. One boy approached Parker, shook hands with him, and said, "Man, I've never had a class like this one. You are great!" One of the girls, a mousey-appearing sort who sat in the back of the room but who had summoned the courage to express an opinion on slavery and discrimination toward the end of class, gave Parker a note: "Mr. Substitute Teacher: I LOVE YOU! You make everything so EXCITING! and INTERESTING! I WANT to learn from you. PLEASE come back again!!!"

Parker wiped a tear from his eye. He believed he had made a real difference in the lives of those youth.

THE DILEMMA

Parker did not follow the lesson plan prepared for him by Ms. Fellows; however he did interest and inspire the students with the stories he told.

Should Parker be kept on the substitute teacher list?

THE DEBATE

Pro

Of course Parker should be kept on the substitute teacher list, and he should be used as often as possible. Obviously he is a great teacher, the sort of teacher needed in our schools. The question really is: is it better to have students endure a class they dislike intensely day after day, or is it better that for at least one day a gifted teacher makes the class relevant to their lives, interesting, even exciting and inspirational? Is it better to really help kids learn or is it better to slavishly follow a course of study?

If the school district in which Parker subbed could persuade him to return to the classroom full-time, what a great thing that would be, but falling short of that perhaps he could be employed to mentor young teachers like Ms. Fellows, the hope being that they will better understand the needs of their students and what "turns them on" academically.

Con

Although Parker presented an interesting and perhaps inspirational lesson to the students, he should not be retained as a substitute teacher. It is imperative that lesson plans prepared by the regular teacher be followed by the substitute, otherwise no accountability can be established. Were this not so, the substitute could teach anything, even going so far as to indoctrinate students with subversive and dangerous ideas.

Moreover, the continuity of the course is disrupted when the substitute elects not to follow the lesson plan. The regular teacher must spend class time to make up the assigned lesson, thus putting him/her behind in accomplishing what is to be done during the semester.

Another important consideration: by not following the lesson plan and by telling the stories he told, Parker damaged Ms. Fellows's relationship with her students. After his "entertaining performance" they will not be pleased nor content with Ms. Fellows as their teacher. She will experience more discipline problems, and the students are unlikely to fulfill the requirements of the class.

As a teacher with many years experience in the classroom, Parker should have been aware of the responsibilities of substitute teachers, the first and foremost of those responsibilities being that they follow the lesson plan.

Parker should definitely not be used further as a substitute teacher.

THE RESOLUTION

Parker subbed no more in that district's schools. Two days after the experience described he received a letter from the district's Director of Curriculum. It read in part: "You are hereby notified that your name has been removed from the list of available substitute teachers in the city's public schools, the reason being that you did not follow the lesson plan provided."

TWO
Arturo's Eligibility

Arturo came to the East Bay Pirate High School from a school in Los Angeles. Enrolled as a junior, he was sent off to classes, notably to Mr. Headley's history class, the only section with a vacancy.

Arturo soon found a friend, Pete, a senior, who, like Arturo, spoke Spanish at home and thus could easily converse with Arturo, who spoke and understood only a little English. Pete, an outstanding cross-country runner himself, soon discovered that Arturo had some running ability, too. Pete suggested to Arturo that he become a member of the cross-country team, a prospect that delighted Arturo as well as pleased Coach Boston when he timed the new boy and found he could run nearly as fast as Pete.

Before every cross-country meet an eligibility slip had to be signed by each athlete's instructor to be turned in to the Dean of Boys, Mr. Battier.

Arturo's problem? Mr. Headley gave a quiz at the end of each week. How could Arturo pass the quizzes? He read English poorly, and the dates and places from the class lectures baffled him completely. He would be ineligible.

But, a solution. As a junior the previous year Pete had been in Mr. Headley's class. He had saved his quizzes to review for the final test. He still had the quizzes, and he guessed that Mr. Headley changed the quiz questions very little from year to year.

Therefore, Pete drilled Arturo on the answers to the quiz questions.

At first all went well, but then Mr. Headley began to suspect something. How could Arturo do so well when his English was so poor? Hmm.

Thus, Mr. Headley changed the questions on the next quiz. Arturo answered only six of twenty questions correctly. Clearly, it appeared to Mr. Headley, the youth had cheated on the previous quizzes.

Mr. Headley sent Arturo's eligibility slip to Mr. Battier, the Dean of Boys, with the word "Ineligible" scrawled across it in big red letters, along with the word "Cheated" immediately below it.

The policy with respect to ineligible athletes was that the dean would notify the coach of the affected sport that the student was ineligible. Without such notification the coach would assume his athlete was eligible.

Somehow Dean Battier forgot to notify Coach Boston of Arturo's ineligibility.

Thus Arturo ran in the conference meet — and won the race, even beating Pete. By a single point, the Pirates retained the conference cross-country title for an eighth year in a row.

Hearing of Arturo's triumph in the cross-country meet, Mr. Headley marched down to Dean Battier's office and demanded to know why Arturo had been permitted to run. Dean Battier sorted through the eligibility slips from the week before. Arturo's eligibility slip seemed to be missing. Dean Battier went through the slips again. No eligibility slip. A third time through he located the offending slip stuck right on the underside of Pete's slip.

Certain that Pete and Arturo had conspired to hide the slip, Mr. Headley demanded that both boys be properly punished. Dean Battier agreed. He removed Arturo from Mr. Headley's class and enrolled him in Ms. Jensen's section where a vacancy had opened. Moreover, he promised to report the matter to Coach Boston who would no doubt feel obligated to forfeit his team's win because an ineligible boy had run. And finally, the dean promised to advise Arturo's parents to counsel their son to respect honesty more and study harder.

In fact Dean Battier did visit Arturo's parents — to congratulate them on their son's work ethic that permitted him to excel in cross-country. He also visited Coach Boston to congratulate him on his team's performance. Somehow he entirely forgot to mention anything about Arturo's eligibility.

Believing he had extracted his pound of flesh, Mr. Headley carried his complaint no further.

Later in the privacy of his office Dean Battier examined Arturo's eligibility slip. He could barely make out the four tiny spots of glue affixing it to the underside of Pete's slip. The dean looked down at the small bottle of glue in his desk drawer. He smiled.

The year passed. Arturo learned English. The next cross-country season he led the Pirates to the conference championship again.

Mr. Headley continued to teach history.

THE DILEMMA

Dean Battier clearly acted to permit Arturo to run in the conference cross-country meet despite school policy, which stated that any student-athlete who failed to maintain a passing grade in any class should be declared ineligible and thus should not be permitted to compete until he/she achieved a passing grade.

Actually here we have not one dilemma, but rather two or even three, the first and most important being the deliberate decision of Dean Battier not to follow established school policy. Should this decision be discovered by Dean Battier's superiors—the school's principal, members of the board of education—even by the cross-country coach or by Mr. Headley, how should Dean Battier then be disciplined, if at all? Remember, Dean Battier's action, or rather inaction, had enabled the Pirates to win the conference championship.

The second dilemma: Arturo knowingly cheated to achieve a satisfactory grade on the first group of quizzes. How should this matter be handled?

The third dilemma: Pete conspired with Arturo to help the latter maintain his eligibility.

How should Pete's actions be addressed?

THE DEBATE

Pro

Dean Battier should not have been disciplined at all. What did he do that was so wrong? He allowed a shy boy who spoke little English to excel in one of the very few areas in school in which he could excel, cross-country. Quite likely Arturo's cross-country victory gave him confidence that he could succeed and set him on the path toward success in other areas of life.

No doubt Dean Battier asked himself several questions that day when he chose to "misplace" Mr. Headley's slip denying Arturo eligibility to participate in the cross-country meet.

Among those questions: had Arturo done anything to warrant being denied his opportunity to run that day, anything over which he had control? The answer: nothing. He could not understand English well enough to grasp the lessons. Assume Mr. Headley had been transported to Saudi Arabia and told he would be punished should he not pass a test given in Arabic. Would it be right and just that he be punished? Of course not. In that situation Mr. Headley might possibly have found a Saudi friend who through some subterfuge could help him.

Another question: would Arturo have been helped toward success in life by being kept from running? No, quite the opposite. He would have resented being punished for something over which he had no immediate control. Recognizing the injustice of the punishment he might have turned from a healthy social activity, a high school sport, to join a gang.

Moreover, had Arturo been prevented from participating in the cross-country meet, other members of the team, recognizing the obvious inability of Arturo to pass the history test given his language handicap, would have strongly resented the school's eligibility policy, and certainly they would have blamed Mr. Headley and even Dean Battier for their loss of the conference title.

To be sure, the actions of the school administrators were flawed from the beginning by enrolling Arturo in Mr. Headley's class. His language difficulties should have been recognized, and he should have been placed in an intensive ESL program. Failing that, Mr. Headley should have recognized Arturo's needs in the first weeks of school and should have communicated his concerns to Dean Battier, the principal, and the appropriate counselor then.

With regard to the second and third dilemmas, the actions of Arturo and Pete in conspiring to hoodwink Mr. Headley, what they did might be considered improper in that they were, indeed, cheating if that word is held to the closest definition. The reason for their cheating is analogous to the reason for shoplifting a loaf of bread if one is starving.

It may be argued that the worst culprit in this matter was Mr. Headley. Not only did he do nothing to help Arturo learn, but he was also at fault for giving the same quizzes year after year. Certainly more students than Pete recognized this and thus they, too, "cheated."

Finally it appears that Mr. Headley was a teacher who took pleasure in "entrapment." Rather than dealing sensibly with Arturo's comprehension problem, he found a way to "get" the young man, possibly because he—Mr. Headley—disliked athletes.

Con

Disgusting! Disgraceful! Dishonest! Dean Battier displayed an appalling lack of ethics. Should his deceit have been discovered by any school official he should have been dismissed from his position immediately. The school's policy that an athlete must attain a "C" average before being permitted to participate in his/her sport should have been followed to the letter. Extracurricular activities are just that, extracurricular, and grade policies relating to participation should not be ignored or subverted in the interest of athletic success.

Consider the results of Dean Battier's perfidy. The second-place team, the rightful winner of the cross-country meet, was denied their victory. The second-place runner was cheated of his win by an ineligible opponent. The Pirate team won an undeserved victory, thereby causing them to exult in a triumph not truly theirs.

In Mr. Headley's eyes both Arturo and Pete surely came to be considered cheaters. While neither was involved in the matter of the "misplaced" eligibility slip, both were, in truth, cheaters in that they contrived to use Mr. Headley's previous year's quizzes to enable Arturo to get through the first few weeks of the class with passing grades.

Without question Arturo and Pete learned a most destructive lesson: that cheaters do win. No doubt each became more amenable to finding moral and ethical shortcuts in other aspects of life. As well, surely other members of Arturo's class must have realized that he could not have been passing with a "C" or above grade. They, too, like Arturo and Pete, may have become more inclined to excuse their own unethical behavior.

School policies are set for good reason in most cases. Policies relating to athletic eligibility are among those set for very good reasons. They must be recognized and obeyed.

THE RESOLUTION

In this case, there was no clear resolution. No one knew of Dean Battier's "noble ignoring of the policy," or " duplicity in concealing the ineligibility of an athlete," depending on which view of his action one embraces.

It may be argued that his decision to let Arturo participate proved to be the right decision. Thirty-one years after the incident, as one of the school's honored faculty, Dean Battier, then retired, attended a Pirate reunion. Before dinner Arturo, by then a Spanish teacher in another high school in the area, visited with Dean Battier, shook his hand, and said, "Thanks for what you did for me when I ran cross-country my junior year. I've never forgotten that."

But wait a minute. It cannot really be known what effect Dean Battier's malfeasance had on others: the other students in the history class, the members of the second place team, Pete, Mr. Headley, and even Dean Battier himself.

Perhaps, by their very nature, some dilemmas can never really be resolved.

THREE
History Taught "Backward"

In her days as a high school and college student, Sunny Copeland followed the standard chronological method of learning American history. She learned the Presidents in order well enough. She remembered historical dates quite well.

But—big question for Ms. Copeland when she became a high school teacher herself: *how* had the threatened impeachment of Richard Nixon, for example, made any difference to her students? How are people impacted by historical events?

Thus, in her third year of teaching in a small Midwestern school, she decided to change her method of teaching history. She would begin at the present *and work backward.* In other words, we are in this situation now; how did we get there?

And at the end of the project, the really important question the student ideally would ask himself/herself: how does this present situation either actually or potentially affect me?

Reasoning that children like mysteries, she assigned "history mysteries" to be solved.

For example, she might assign this "mystery to be solved:" why is the United States in Iraq? The students would then "proceed" backward from ISIS to 9/11 to weapons of mass destruction to a plot to assassinate the first President Bush to the British protectorate to Kurds, Shias, and Sunnis, and even to the question of who should succeed the Prophet Mohammed when he died.

Thus Ms. Copeland's students learned the ultimate reason for our being in Iraq and how that affected them.

Uncovering what the past held led to eager and intense detective work by the students. And as the pieces of the puzzles were assembled into a whole, students engaged in animated discussions about what caused what, and how much the cause did or did not create the subsequent effect.

Yes, believed Ms. Copeland, backward was the best method of teaching history. Not cause to effect, but effect back to cause, to effect back to cause, back to effect . . . ad infinitum (well, not quite) as a means of understanding the present.

Ms. Copeland's students loved her classes. They were fun, and they learned, too.

For six years all went well for Ms. Sunny Copeland. Then she moved from the small school in which she taught to a big city high school. Before long word got back to the chairman of the school's social studies department that Ms. Sunny Copeland *taught history backward.*

To learn more the chairman visited with students in Ms. Copeland's class. All with whom he spoke liked her method. Very much.

He promptly went into her class to observe her method. Although his first impression of what was happening in the class was positive—the students seemed interested and attentive—he soon recognized the inherent problem with teaching history backward.

He sighed and resigned himself to telling Ms. Copeland she must change her teaching method.

THE DILEMMA

Students who might move from one high school to another in the district during the course of the year might be handicapped because of the difference in teaching methods they encountered—chronological as opposed to non-chronological. Would this be fair to a student who moved?

Should Ms. Copeland be permitted to teach history backward?

THE DEBATE

Pro

The only valid reason to teach American history is to enable students to have an understanding of America's past and *how the past is relevant to them and to their future.*

The biggest complaint of high school students is that certain required courses are *not* relevant to their lives. While they may not understand how such courses are relevant, it is the job of the teacher to help them understand relevancy. This is undeniably made easier if the unit of study is based on the students' present, the here and now, and moved back into the past to illustrate how the present came to be and how it impacts the students' lives.

This understanding is vitally important to America's flourishing as a democracy. When citizens give up in substantial numbers and do not vote, take as little notice of government as possible, are swayed in their beliefs by demagogues or cynically believe that all governments are inevitably corrupt, America is well on the road to disaster.

The argument that the traditional chronological teaching of American history is the best method does not stand up to scrutiny. A very large majority of Americans, all of whom have suffered through the usual recitation of events, dates, and places in history classes, have very limited knowledge of this country's history.

Select at random ten adults on the street and ask them the significance of any five important historical events in American history—let us say, for example, the battle of Yorktown, the Constitutional Convention, the Monroe Doctrine, the Treaty of Versailles, and the Civil Rights Bill of 1964—and not more than one of the ten will be able to give a satisfactory answer to more than one or two of the events cited. Indeed, most will have no idea what you are talking about. As it is taught traditionally in high schools, studying the history of this nation is largely a useless exercise.

The essential point is: learning must be relevant to students; really, of course, to anyone. It must mean something that can be used for life activities beyond the playing of *Jeopardy*, and Ms. Copeland's teaching backward method is an excellent way to make American history relevant. (Indeed, her method should be taught to *all* teachers of American history. It is that important.)

Con

Ms. Sunny Copeland might be a good teacher, but it is important that she follow the district's course of study. Why? Because in a large district many students will move around within the district. They will not be in only one school all of the semester, but will transfer from one school to another for various reasons. Thus, a student who is in School A in which Ms. Sunny teaches "backward history" and moves to School B in which history is taught in the traditional way will be hopelessly lost. This means that it will be difficult, if not impossible, to determine an objective grade for the student. For this reason if no other, it is important to have teachers of all sections of any subject on roughly the same page.

Moreover, there is no reason that history taught in a chronological manner cannot be made interesting. Washington's winter at Valley Forge is interesting in and of itself. It need not be tied to some other barely similar event in the discussion of America's wars. The good and bad of Presidential administrations stand of and by themselves; they need not be linked to the scandals of the Nixon administration—because they are, in fact, not related.

Finally, it is hard to believe that Ms. Copeland's method will enable the students to cover all that should be covered in a semester or year of history. Indeed, simply because time marches on and more and more history is created, it is difficult to cover all that should be covered through the chronological method. Because they have not been taught all they should have been taught during the time allotted, Ms. Copeland's students will test at a lower level than students taught in the conventional way.

Ms. Copeland should be afforded the opportunity to change her teaching method, but if she cannot or will not do that, she should then be terminated.

THE RESOLUTION

None of the administrative officials at the school or in the district were ever forced to resolve the matter.

Asked to change her teaching method to the more traditional chronological method, Ms. Copeland did try to change. A minor disaster ensued. Students demanded she revert to her "backward" way. With the very reluctant acquiescence of the social studies department chairman she did but only for the remainder of the first semester.

Before the start of the spring semester Ms. Sunny Copeland took a position in a small private school in the same city at three-fourths her previous salary.

And she continued to teach history backward.

FOUR
Homework—Yes or No

Bill Larsen and Trey Wall both were in their third year of teaching at Middletown High—Bill in math, Trey in family finance. Both were married, and the two couples often played cards together on Saturday evenings.

Bill lamented after one card game that he still had homework papers to grade. This led Amanda, Trey's wife, to say she saw no value in homework, that her homework assignments taught her little and caused her to resent the class and the teacher.

Amanda's statement led to a larger discussion of the value of homework. The four agreed that most homework had a negative effect on many students.

Thinking about it a day or two later Trey hatched a new and different idea for homework.

Because school policy dictated that homework must be assigned, he did not abandon the practice, but he did change it significantly.

After discussing the matter of homework with his students—they disliked doing it even more than he disliked grading it—he trotted out his "homework but different" idea. He would assign homework, but not necessarily homework on the topic being studied in class.

Instead the students would work on, as one student, put it, "whatever floats our boats."

In other words, within limits and with certain ground rules, students could choose a topic of their own interest to research and report on.

Among the ground rules Trey set: students must spend at least three hours a week on their research. Their research must be done in a scientific manner, no "I think" or "it seems to me" sorts of conclusions. All research must be on "legal" topics, no digging into how to make bombs, nothing like that. Above all, the research must be based on something they believed could actually benefit them in the future—in their careers, in their leisure, in their family life—and, finally, something about which they had some genuine passion.

Before starting their "homework," each student would be expected to meet with Trey and have him approve his or her topic. If he disapproved, another topic must be chosen. Trey would meet with each student once every two weeks to discuss their ongoing research. All would submit a paper detailing their research conclusions at the end of the semester.

And, one more thing, the students must agree to "really bear down in class and learn about family finance," the actual subject of the class being taught.

The students agreed to all of it. Enthusiastically they agreed because they believed themselves now free to work on whatever, as the student had earlier put it, "floated their boats."

The experiment began well. Parents, most of whom had themselves had an aversion to homework in their student days, even those who initially were skeptical, soon embraced the program, pleased that their teens were doing significant and meaningful "homework" without being dragooned into it.

Some students came up with information and knowledge they were excited about putting to use in the near future. By the end of the fall semester a bright young man named Harv Clark had begun a business called Gridiron Metrics which he touted as a service to provide in-depth analysis to high school and college football coaches on a variety of game situations; e.g., "if my team faces fourth and three at our own thirty-five yard line, based on statistical information, should I punt or run a slant off-tackle to try to pick up the first down." Harv claimed his researched information would open a coach's eyes to a whole set of possibilities and probabilities he could then use to improve his team's performance.

Several of the other students' research projects showed promise, too. One student, a young man who enjoyed cooking, created several tasty recipes with his homework.

Trey believed his *"relevance"* homework assignment had worked very well.

THE DILEMMA

The school principal, having learned of Trey's homework practice, although sympathetic to his objectives, said that a few parents, a very few, but some, objected to the fact that no homework was being done on the real subject of the class, family finance.

In addition, a few of the faculty had complained that their students, still confined to traditional homework, resented their fellow students' (those in Mr. Wall's class) being permitted to do their homework on "something fun."

Perhaps, the principal strongly suggested, Trey should return to a more traditional type of homework based on material more directly applicable to family finance.

The question then: should Trey Wall return to the traditional homework assignments closely dealing with the class subject?

THE DEBATE

Pro

Homework is a topic on which there has been much debate and much written recently. There are plenty of positive reasons for the continuation of the traditional model of homework as long as (1) it has a close relevance to classroom teaching, (2) it provides a means by which the teacher may offer feedback to the student, and (3) it offers the student a means to better understand not only the lesson being taught but ideally how that lesson fits into a larger scheme of things.

The "homework method" adopted by Mr. Wall and his students may be better than simply abandoning homework assignments altogether; however, there are several things wrong with it.

First, it is not really homework at all. Rather the student is doing research and often, usually probably, not at all in the subject area of the class. The student may learn nothing that will be of value to him in the subject area. While the student may do research with a good deal of passion on his "self-selected homework," it will advance his knowledge of family finance very little. Facts and concepts learned through homework, done properly, can provide information and understanding useful and necessary to the lessons of life.

Moreover, a student working with Mr. Wall's model may have a distorted and unrealistic interest in that which they are researching, thus using time which might be better spent on a productive lesson from the classroom topic. For example, middle school boys may "know" they are going to be sports stars when in truth few will ever make the roster of a college sports team. However, had a teacher permitted them free rein with their homework a la Wall's system, many would have opted for some type of research about sports. Through their research few would have learned much about family finance which is, after all, a rather important subject.

One more thing: homework done correctly requires diligence, doggedness, and determination. The student must buckle down and "get 'er done," as Larry the Cable Guy would say. The willingness to "get 'er done" is a big part of success in life. Not every task in life is going to fit into the student's passion. Many are bluntly hard slogs that must be accomplished. Traditional homework assignments help instill the "get 'er done" quality in youth.

The whole question of homework value comes down to good teachers. A good teacher will be able to assign homework interesting and relevant to the student. That is really the be all and the end all of the matter.

Con

For starters let's go to Bill Gates, Larry Page, Mark Zuckerberg, and Warren Buffett and ask them what they gained from doing assigned homework. The bet is that none of them can remember much at all learned from class-assigned homework

On the other hand, Gates, Page, and Zuckerberg *did* learn a great deal from exercising their passion for computers, while Buffett profited greatly from his interest in business matters.

Well, okay, we won't ask Gates et al. Instead we will ask half a hundred "ordinary" citizens. What will their evaluations be of the homework done by them in middle school and high school? We suggest the responses would often be: "Hated homework." "Taught me nothing." "My mom mostly did it." "I just ignored it; my teacher didn't care, less for him to grade."

Almost all of the research done relating to the value of homework shows that only in the lower elementary grades does it contribute to learning. Homework assigned to middle school students and high school students has very little positive effect, and for many students, has a decidedly negative effect.

THE RESOLUTION

Trey Wall sighed mightily and returned to assigning traditional homework.

FIVE
Cullen's Grade?

In addition to teaching at a community college, Eric Evans undertook to teach American history to inmates in a Federal Youth Authority facility. There he had a class of fifteen young men, all between seventeen and twenty-three years old. None had completed high school. All had committed serious crimes, including murder.

On the first day of class Evans gave a multiple choice test to evaluate the students' knowledge of the American past. One student took the test paper and placed it on the floor beside his chair. He did not take the test. He sat quietly and stared into space.

Evans twice asked him to take the test, saying it had nothing to do with a grade. The student did not respond. A second student explained the non-action of the first, saying, "That's Cullen. He won't take the test. He believes he's unjustly incarcerated so he's taken a vow of silence while he's here. He won't say a word to anyone. We call him Sullen Cullen."

During the first class Cullen responded to nothing. As soon as the class ended, Evans went to the Education Officer at the facility to learn more about the mute student.

"Oh, yes," the officer responded. "That's Cullen. I should have told you about him. He never speaks. He won't participate in class, but don't worry. He's harmless. He won't bother you or any of the other inmates."

Evans asked, "So how will I grade him?"

The Education Officer shrugged. "Give him what grade you'd like. Personally, I'd suggest you give him a C. His grade will never matter to him or to anyone else."

As the class went on Evans came to accept Cullen's behavior. In one class period a discussion arose about the importance of youth finding good role models. An inmate charged with a Mann Act violation defended the value of role models. Another contended that role models were only for youth who could not face "being themselves."

At various points in the discussion Evans thought he caught Sullen Cullen shaking his head in disagreement, or in another instance barely cracking a smile, a disdainful smile to be sure but at least a facial expression. Evans asked Cullen if he wanted to contribute something to the discussion. Cullen immediately resumed his blank countenance.

At other times Evans thought Cullen almost on the verge of speaking, but he did not. Not once during the entire semester did he say a word.

On the last day of class Evans thanked the inmates for their interest and participation. They, in turn, thanked him. One of the class members recited a few appropriate remarks about how much they had enjoyed the class. Others chimed in with their thanks to Evans.

All except Sullen Cullen who sat unmoving, expressionless, in his usual chair.

The students left the classroom ahead of Evans. He trailed them down the hall. A few feet out of the room Evans sensed a presence back of his right shoulder. Cullen. He had not left the room with the others. For a brief second Evans nearly panicked, the thought of a shiv being driven into his back.

Sullen Cullen stepped close to Evans, his head turned to the teacher's ear. He broke his long silence. He whispered gruffly into Evan's ear. "Hey, man, you're okay."

He hurried ahead to catch up with the other inmates.

When he recorded the final grades for his prisoner students, Evans wondered what effect he had had, or ever would have, on the life of the inmate Cullen.

THE DILEMMA

What grade does Evans give the student who never spoke in class, who never took a test or handed in a paper.

Perhaps, he thought, he should give Cullen a C just as the Education Officer had suggested. The young man had caused no troubles. He had listened.

THE DEBATE

Pro

Evans should give Cullen a passing grade, perhaps not an A, perhaps a C just as suggested. Evans has no certain knowledge of what Cullen actually learned in class. It is entirely possible that after the class Cullen's knowledge of American history—and of life— exceeded that of the students who received high grades. Evans does not and cannot know.

Why does the grade given any of the inmates matter at all? When they are released from prison and seek employment no prospective employer will place any importance on the grade they received in an American history class while incarcerated. None at all.

One last point: if Evans were to give Cullen a D or an F, Cullen's resentment of the justice system would grow. A higher grade, a C or even a B, might provide Cullen evidence that he might be treated justly, at least some times by some people.

A glimmer of hope for Cullen was manifested in his words to Evans.

Cut the youth some slack when grading him.

Con

Cullen took none of the tests; he never said a word in class; and yet because of one sentence, barely a full sentence, Evans is thinking of giving him a passing grade. That is *really* grade inflation.

There is little else to say. By any measure, Cullen should receive an F.

THE RESOLUTION

After considering the matter for two days and asking the counsel of several other teachers, the facility's Education Officer, and his own wife, Evans recorded a B for Cullen.

SIX
Bernie's Grade?

Because her husband's work forced a move to another city, long-time teacher Kathleen Schremp left her previous school and found a position in a high school in the new city.

Ms. Schremp taught economics, and she taught in a no nonsense way. At the first meeting of her classes she instructed her students as to what was expected of them along these lines: Get your assignments done fully and promptly. Study for the tests. Be present. Do not miss class.

She graded strictly. Ninety-seven to one hundred equaled an A plus, a grade few of her students achieved. Seventy-three to seventy-six equaled a C, a grade many of her students achieved. She accepted few excuses for poor performance. Students were held accountable for everything asked on a test. She prided herself on treating all students alike, no discrimination.

The first day of class in her new school went well. One student, a young man named Bernie Gleason, particularly impressed Ms. Schremp. He appeared to be quite knowledgeable, not only in economics, but in more general areas, too.

As the class went on, Ms. Schremp became more and more impressed by Bernie's knowledge and his ability to express what he knew. Surprisingly for a high school senior, he had read Adam Smith's *Wealth of Nations*. He understood Malthusian theory. He defended Jeremy Bentham's Utilitarianism. He provided cogent arguments supporting or attacking various economic theories. He debated Arthur Leffler's "trickle down" ideas with other students. Ms. Schremp believed Bernie Gleason to be the best economics student she had ever taught.

Then, halfway through the course, she gave Major Test Number One. She chose five questions to ask her students. They were to write on three of the five.

Ms. Schremp eagerly awaited Bernie's paper. He took the entire hour allotted for the test. She supposed he must be answering all five questions or else he was writing virtual dissertations on the three he had chosen to answer.

At the end of class he folded his papers, handed in his answers, and fled from the classroom. Puzzled by his swift exit, Ms. Schremp unfolded his papers, five in all.

Bernie Gleason had scrawled a large, nearly indecipherable sentence on each paper. Just one sentence.

Utterly astonished and shocked, Ms. Schremp sat motionless at her desk for several minutes. What had happened? How could her prize student, the one who could hold forth on economic theories for hours, how could he have blown the test so completely? Could he have been on drugs? Could he have suffered some type of seizure? What on earth could have happened?

She graded the other students' papers but put no grade on Bernie's abominable effort. The next day she called Bernie into her office and asked him to explain what had happened. Very nervous, he replied, "No excuse. I didn't study." That was all. He looked down at his shoes and quickly left her office.

She felt she had no choice. She put a large red F on his paper.

In the next day's class, Bernie again rose to the fore in oral discussion. He knew everything from the assigned chapter. Moreover, he added pertinent information of his own.

After class, Ms. Schremp again sat at her desk, more puzzled than ever. Well, she decided, perhaps Bernie's previous teachers knew something about him she did not know. She walked down to the office of Adams, a math teacher, and started her question by saying, "I have a student in my class named Bernie Gleason . . ."

Upon hearing the name, Adams interrupted, nodding, and saying, "I know what you are going to ask me. You gave a major test, and Bernie earned a big fat F."

Adams continued, "I'm surprised no one told you about Bernie before. You should have been warned. Bernie is one of the top five students in this school, maybe the absolute best when it comes to knowing a subject and being able to discuss it . . . orally. Bernie cannot write."

Adams went on to explain Bernie's problem. "He suffers from a neurological condition called dysgraphia. Whereas dyslexia impairs the ability to read, dysgraphia impairs the ability to write. Bernie is absolutely brilliant, no question about it, but he cannot put his knowledge down on paper. He's very self-conscious and sensitive about his problem. He doesn't want to talk about it, or even admit he has it."

THE DILEMMA

The dilemma is simple: what grade should Ms. Schremp assign Bernie Gleason? Should she give him a failing grade based on his inability to write anything on the midterm test?

THE DEBATE

Pro

Regrettably, Ms. Schremp must give Bernie a failing grade. She instructed students at the time of the first class meeting of the grading standard. Major tests were to be fifty percent of their final grade.

The ability to write well is of crucial importance in working in today's world. That vital avenue to successful communication is closed to Bernie.

Of course Ms. Schremp doubtless feels sympathy for Bernie. So would any other caring teacher. However, students must be evaluated on what they actually do and not on what they are perhaps capable of doing. Their grades should not be inflated because teachers are sympathetic toward them and *wish* they could do more.

Other teachers coming before Ms. Schremp have not done Bernie any favors by passing him along despite his handicap. In all likelihood Bernie will go into the world of work and will be hired because most human resource managers will be impressed by his evident intelligence, his oral communication skills, and his social skills. He will be hired, but soon his supervisors will realize that he cannot transfer his thoughts from mind to paper or screen, and he will be dismissed, reluctantly—sadness all the way around, but he will be gone.

At all levels of education teachers must shoulder the responsibility of evaluating students honestly. The high school basketball coach who assures his six-foot, three-inch center that he can be a star in the NBA is doing the boy a disservice. The English teacher who encourages her C student that she can become a best-selling novelist is leading the student down the road to rejection and disappointment.

No, the big red F Ms. Schremp put on Bernie's midterm paper is entirely appropriate . . . and necessary.

Con

The argument that Bernie cannot have a highly successful career because of his inability to put thoughts on paper is entirely specious. Plenty of careers are open to someone with a high intellect, the ability to speak effectively, and, save for his reluctance to discuss his handicap, excellent social skills.

A teacher who has a student restricted to a wheelchair does not lower the student's grade because he cannot walk. Neither should the grade of a neurologically handicapped student be lowered.

Ms. Schremp should have been apprised of Bernie's handicap before the first day of class. His counselors and former teachers knew he could not write.

But once she knew of his disability Ms. Schremp should have discussed the problem with Bernie's parents, with counselors, with other faculty members, but she should not fail the boy because of his disability.

THE RESOLUTION

Ms. Schremp did discuss the matter of Bernie's dysgraphia with other appropriate persons, including his parents.

After a good bit of soul searching, she gave Bernie a final grade of A-plus.

SEVEN

The Trumpet Thief

As an East Bay High School junior Bobby Oman chose to defy most authority.

If he believed he had been disrespected by a teacher, he might depict that teacher in an unfavorable light in graffiti on the back wall of the high school. Or in class if he disagreed with another student's point of view, he might bark loud yelps of dismay.

Bobby Oman was short in stature—only five-three, and a bit rotund—not obese but somewhat overweight. Some of the teachers in their roles as amateur psychologists believed the youth's perception of his physical shortcomings caused his defiant attitude. He was attempting to compensate for his lack of height and his surplus weight—and thus a lack of athletic ability in a school where athletes were admired and adored.

He was intelligent. He passed his classes with mostly C's but with an occasional A if he thought the class relevant to his life. There were few of the latter.

Teachers hated to have Bobby Oman assigned to their classes.

Directly across the street from the back of the high school in a second story apartment lived Ron Church, a twenty-four-year-old science teacher respected and beloved by his students. A superb athlete, only two years before Mr. Church had come within one place of qualifying for the U.S. Olympic team in the hurdles. Unmarried and with no steady girlfriend, Mr. Church's good looks and friendly manner prompted a few of the high school girls to form a semi-secret fan club called "Romance with Ron." However, on the night to be described it was the young teacher's athletic ability that is pertinent.

On a particularly warm night in March around two in the morning Mr. Church awakened to hear the sound of breaking glass. He rose from his bed and looked out his window toward the school. He saw someone at that very instant reaching through a broken window to unlock the door leading to the music room.

Even in the faint light cast by the street lamp Mr. Church believed he recognized the intruder. Bobby Oman. Hastily Mr. Church slipped on a pair of sweat pants, put on his shoes, and then he paused to consider his options. He could call the police. There had been a break-in at the high school. The culprit was at that very moment still in the music room. The police probably would be in time to catch him.

On the other hand, Mr. Church believed he knew the identity of the intruder. Bobby Oman. He rather liked Bobby. Oh, yes, Bobby could be a load, however, he was intelligent and quite witty really. And talented. The graffiti he drew on walls (though he had been sly enough never to be caught) imitating the British graffiti artist Banksy showed real artistic ability.

Mr. Church trotted down a flight of stairs to the apartment's outer door. He waited briefly. Soon Bobby Oman appeared, pushing through the door of the music room with an instrument case in his hand. He started down the street in a lively walk.

Mr. Church opened the apartment door and yelled at Bobby to stop. Bobby did not stop but broke into a run. The teacher who had tried out for the Olympic team had no trouble catching him. Bobby struggled. Mr. Church subdued him, and with the old arm-behind-the-back, come-along-with-me hold marched Bobby back to his apartment building and up the stairs to his room.

For two hours Mr. Church talked to Bobby Oman, first with a barrage of questions: "What in the name of God is wrong with you, Bobby? You are smart, in fact, gifted; why do you want to risk all you have? You can be somebody, Bobby. You do not need to be the ultimate screw up. Why?" Like that.

Bobby sat on the bed and sobbed out his remorse.

He tried to explain he had stolen the trumpet (the instrument in the case) because he wanted to be in a band just forming, and he had no money to buy an instrument.

Mr. Church barked at him to shut up.

At seven that morning Mr. Church loaded Bobby into his car and drove him to McDonald's for a quick breakfast.

They returned to school. Bobby walked down the hall to the principal's office, trumpet case in hand, Mr. Church two steps behind. Bobby politely asked the secretary if he might speak to Mr. Schneider, the principal.

Bobby put the trumpet on Mr. Schneider's desk and confessed, "Sir, I stole this last night, and I also did some damage to the back door into the music room. I know what I did was wrong. I want to return this trumpet, and I will pay for the window I broke. I hope you'll let me stay in school and not call the police."

THE DILEMMA

Here we have two dilemmas really, the first being: should Mr. Ron Church have confronted the thief Bobby Oman; the second being: how should the principal Mr. Schneider have responded to Bobby's plea to stay in school?

THE DEBATE

Pro

Yes, given the facts as presented, Ron Church acted properly in accosting Bobby Oman.

The young teacher was very athletic. Therefore, it was unlikely that the short, overweight Bobby represented any physical threat to him. The youth was not going to be able to punch him and knock him down—nothing like that.

More importantly, if Bobby were arrested and convicted, he might be sent to a facility where he would be the object of uninvited and undeserved physical assaults. As it was pointed out, he was intelligent and witty. Clearly he knew the break-in was wrong. But he saw no other way to get an instrument so that he might be in a band, apparently a very important desire—and even need—for him and his dream of a brighter future where he would be known not for his back wall graffiti, but for his musical ability.

To his great credit Mr. Church did not call the police. He did what any parent or surrogate parent should, but too often doesn't, do. He "tough loved" Bobby to show him the error of his ways and show him why he should change. And how he could change.

And he bought the boy breakfast.

Now to Mr. Schneider's dilemma.

Given the fact that Bobby Oman has never been in trouble with the law before, it seems that the principal should accept Bobby's solemn promise to "change his ways," especially when his promise is believed and supported by Mr. Church.

Con

Let us consider this matter reasonably. Should Ron Church have confronted Bobby Oman after Bobby committed a serious crime, a felony? We know that Bobby dislikes teachers, at least some teachers. He might have especially disliked one who attempted to stop him after he had broken into the high school (and also one who was athletic, handsome, and the subject of female attention, all of which Bobby was not). If Bobby had had a gun, which he well might have, Mr. Church ran a very real risk of being shot and killed.

Criminals are to be dealt with by officers of the law, not by public school teachers. Instead of attempting to confront Bobby, clearly a dangerous and probably useless act, Mr. Church should have called the police as quickly as possible and alerted them to a break-in at the high school.

With regard to Mr. Schneider's decision whether to let Bobby Oman stay in school: here we have a young man who admitted to breaking and entering . . . and theft. One of a school principal's first and most important responsibilities is to cooperate with law enforcement to make his school an orderly place of learning. If he forgives Bobby and exacts no punishment he then opens himself up to criticism and worse, to lawsuits, if and when Bobby commits other crimes.

Moreover, if Bobby is given no punishment, will he not then be more likely to commit further crimes? Is not punishment meant to correct criminal actions?

The principal should decree some penalty. What that penalty ought to be should be decided by the principal in consultation with other appropriate persons, but there should be a penalty.

THE RESOLUTION

We already know what Mr. Ron Church did, whether we agree with what he did or not.

With regard to what Mr. Schneider decided: after initially being quite reluctant to let Bobby off with merely the apology and the promise to pay for the broken window, the principal agreed to Bobby's plea.

Other faculty and support staff members were not informed of Bobby's actions. Mr. Church fibbed by telling those who asked that he had heard the window break, and it had turned out that probably someone had hurled a baseball through the window. . . although none of the custodians found a baseball when they cleaned up the broken glass.

In the weeks after the incident, some teachers who had Bobby Oman in their classes came into the teachers' lounge and shook their heads, mystified that the young man, so disruptive and odious in the past, now acted politely and maintained top grades.

Passing strange, they thought.

EIGHT
Charley's Boy

Coach Charley McGraw's Foster Firebirds, the freshman football team at Foster High School, completed an unbeaten season mainly through the effort of one boy on one play. Down by two points in the last two minutes of the game, Kenny Munson danced and darted his way sixty-five yards to the winning touchdown.

Later in the year the game's hero, the selfsame Kenny Munson, was apprehended after stealing a bottle of vodka from a liquor store. Kenny listened to a fiery lecture from the policeman who caught him, a man who coincidentally had a son who started for the Foster Firebirds. The vodka was returned to the store and no charges were filed.

Mr. Al Franton, the school principal, hearing of the vodka theft and knowing that Kenny had been in minor scrapes before, went to Coach McGraw with the thought that the coach might "take Kenny under his wing" and tutor him, become almost a surrogate parent what with Kenny coming from a single parent household and leading an unstable home life.

THE DILEMMA

Coach McGraw immediately recognized certain problems that might ensue were he to agree to tutor Kenny Munson, the first being that other students and faculty members who learned of the relationship between coach and player would believe it was arranged solely to preserve Kenny's availability to play football for the upcoming three years of high school. This belief would be furthered by the fact that he, Coach McGraw, had already been named the high school's head coach for the coming season, the previous varsity coach having announced his retirement.

Were there not other students, a number of them, whose home lives were worse than Kenny Munson's? Yes, there were. Should they not be provided tutors? Why should Kenny have the benefit of tutoring while other, more deserving students, did not?

Oh, yes, the coach knew, the perception would be that he was spoon-feeding Kenny Munson so the running back would be there for the next three years to run the ball for him and thus elevate his standing in the ranks of high school football coaches.

On the other hand Kenny Munson *did* need an adult male presence in his life. His mother, single, with five other children, could help him little. And, Coach McGraw was sure that Kenny would be offered college scholarships because of his athletic ability if he could be kept away from gangs and out of trouble.

Coach McGraw pondered the matter. Should he agree to tutor Kenny Munson, become almost a surrogate father to the boy?

THE DEBATE

Pro

Of course, Coach McGraw should agree to tutor Kenny Munson irrespective of what others may think and say. The boy needs help and direction. The coach can provide it. While the coach cannot tutor every youth in the school who needs help, at least he can provide help for one youth, one who otherwise probably will join a gang and be embroiled in more serious criminal activity.

Save the kid!

This is not even a close call.

Con

After the shoplifting of the vodka incident, Kenny should have been exposed to the juvenile court system. When he received no punishment and when it was suggested that Coach McGraw tutor him, naturally Kenny believed, correctly, that the tutoring was done to be sure he would be available to play football in upcoming seasons. He recognized his ability, and he knew the coaches and fans recognized it, too. He knew he was "special," therefore he accepted that he would be treated as "special."

Instead of being "scared straight," Kenny is to be rewarded with a tutor. Had he not been a potential star running back, he never would have been afforded special treatment. The coach knows it; the principal knows it; and, for sure, Kenny knows it.

Coach McGraw should not agree to tutor Kenny unless assured that other "at risk" students in the school are afforded the same special treatment.

After all, what is good for the goose should be good for the gander.

THE RESOLUTION

Coach Charley McGraw agreed to tutor Kenny Munson.

All through the winter and into the spring of Kenny's freshman year, Coach McGraw and Kenny met at least two or three times a week to evaluate the boy's academic progress. And there was progress. Kenny's grades improved from D's to C's and even two B's. Other faculty members were aware of Coach McGraw's work with Kenny. Most approved although they all agreed it stemmed from Kenny's excellence on the gridiron. Kenny was better behaved in their classes and seemed to be doing some actual studying.

In early June just before the end of the school year, Kenny came to Coach McGraw one afternoon after classes to ask for help in reviewing for a history test. The two spent two hours reviewing. "Let me know how you do," said the coach as Kenny left. Kenny promised he would.

On Thursday afternoon following the history test Kenny came to Coach McGraw bubbling with pride. He had scored an 89 on the test, the highest grade he had earned during the entire year. He thanked the coach for his help, high fived him, and left the room floating on air.

Upon leaving Coach McGraw after telling of his 89, B-plus, grade, Kenny Munson met an older high school friend, a gang member, who had just received his driver's license. They drove to a nearby town and entered a liquor store. The clerk saw Kenny take the bottle of vodka out the door. He ran after the thief. Kenny pulled a .22 revolver from his belt and shot the clerk, wounding him.

The police caught up with Kenny Munson and his friend five miles down the road.

Coach Charley McGraw started his varsity football coaching duties at Foster High the next fall.

Kenny Munson was not among his players.

NINE
A Jihadist in the School

Liz Daly taught Modern Problems to seniors in an Illinois high school. She also acted in community theater productions. In the course of being an actress she became acquainted with Elwyn Harris, a talented actor who in earlier years had played minor roles in off-Broadway productions.

When the students in Liz's class discussed the role of the United States in the Middle East, one of the boys expressed his wish that a real life jihadist could come to their class to explain why he felt such a fanatical hatred of America.

That gave Ms. Daly an idea. She went to Mr. Harris, a tall man with a dark beard, with the suggestion that he appear in her class pretending to be a jihadist.

Yes, agreed Harris, a capital idea. He would research the extremists' views. He would call a Saudi friend in Chicago who owned Arabic clothing that he never wore and ask if he could borrow some of the clothing. Oh, yes, a capital idea indeed.

THE DILEMMA

Although she initially embraced the idea of Harris-as-a-jihadist, after thinking about the matter for several days, Liz Daly wondered if she had made the right decision. Should she have arranged to have her friend Harris fool her students with a portrayal of a fictional jihadist?

On the one hand the act might cause the students to *really* think seriously about something vitally important, something that *really* did affect them, something more than *Saturday Night Live* or *Dancing with the Stars*.

On the other hand, she wondered, would some of the students develop more empathy and/or sympathy for the jihadists, or at least question

America's role in the Middle East. It was conceivable, wasn't it, she feared, that one or two of her less stable students might be pushed toward such a dislike and distrust of American policies that they might, in fact, commit greater or lesser acts damaging to our country.

Oh, my god! What should she do? Mr. Harris had already called his Chicago friend to arrange to pick up the appropriate clothing.

Should Liz Daly go ahead with the planned deception?

THE DEBATE

Pro

Yes, Ms. Daly should go ahead with the deception. She is doing exactly what a teacher of Modern Problems should do. She is prodding students to examine the problem as thoroughly as possible. Ms. Daly's fear that some of her students are going to be so greatly influenced by the sham jihadist that they may commit treasonous acts is laughable were it not a serious matter. It is certainly possible for students to gain understanding of the rationale for terrorism without agreeing with or condoning the actions of the terrorists.

Foreign policy, or for that matter any sort of policy—government, business, family, any—may be and should be discussed before, during, and after the implementation of the policy.

Given today's Middle Eastern problems directly affecting the United States, it is important that students understand how we came to play the roles that we now play in that part of the world. Americans need to understand the cultural, societal, and religious differences existing between Middle Eastern countries on one hand and American and Western European nations on the other: e.g., the role of women, the notion of jihad, beliefs about the hereafter, and so forth.

While Ms. Daly probably could provide a brief and basic answer to the student's original question about why jihadists hate America, bringing a professional actor to role play will cause her students to be shocked but also to gain greater knowledge and understanding.

Yes, Ms. Daly, go ahead with the deception. It will provide the students with an important lesson they will not forget.

Con

This is a dangerous area that Ms. Daly is thinking about stepping into. If the actor Harris's *shtick* is well done, some students may, indeed, begin to doubt their own government's explanations of reasons for our role in the Middle East. To a degree this is healthy, but carried too far it can and may result in a distrust of American policy, which can and sometimes does lead to violent anti-government acts—e.g., the rise of the posse comitatus; the Ruby Ridge incident of 1992; the raid on the Branch Davidian complex in 1993; and the bombing of the Oklahoma City federal building in 1995.

Some of Ms. Daly's students may come to believe the United States should not have supported the creation of the nation of Israel following World War II, or believe our reason for invading Iraq in 2003 was not the stated reason that Saddam Hussein possessed weapons of mass destruction that presented a danger to us, but rather our desire for more and cheaper oil, or even George W. Bush's "desire to finish the job his father had failed to complete."

Were Ms. Daly to inform her students in advance of the role-playing and, after the Harris performance as a jihadist, had a second skilled actor been made available to present a rebuttal to the jihadist's contentions, that scenario might be acceptable . . . and a valuable lesson.

In any event, Ms. Daly should consult with her principal before going ahead with the Harris presentation.

THE RESOLUTION

While Liz Daly did have qualms about presenting the "jihadist" to her class, Elwyn Harris, now enthusiastic about the idea, convinced her that much good would come from his presentation and no harm.

She thus agreed to have him appear as a real life jihadist.

Mr. Harris thereupon drove to Chicago, about sixty miles, and picked up the *thawb* (a long tunic), the *keffiyeh* (the headdress), and the *agal* (the rope around the headdress).

On the day chosen, Harris strolled into Ms. Daly's fourth period class dressed in his costume, surprising the students considerably. Ms. Daly jumped to her feet to welcome the visitor. She introduced Harris by a Muslim name.

Adopting a Middle Eastern accent, Harris smiled softly and began in a quiet voice, telling the students first about his early life, his education, his love of Islam. Soon he addressed the student's original question: why did he feel such hatred for America?

He began with the creation of the nation of Israel, giving statistics about the number of Palestinians whose land had been taken from them because of American support of a Jewish state. He continued on through the defiling of Muslim lands by American troops, the introduction of lewd and lascivious agents of evil into holy and sacred places in the Islamic world, things like gambling, alcohol, wicked movies, and TV.

Harris hit all of the usual themes of the jihadists. He even explained why music must be banned as well as the drinking of ice water. He emphasized the duty to wage holy war. He warned the students to expect jihad to continue throughout their lives, a war of attrition.

Although Ms. Daly had introduced Harris as a real jihadist, a few of the students initially believed the man could not be a jihadist. Not really. But Harris was an excellent actor.

By the ten minute mark of his lecture a low rumble of disagreement rose from the students. Twenty minutes in as the content of American movies came under fire, a boy shouted, "That's complete bull!" Soon another boy and two girls rose from their desks, said nothing, and left the room. By the thirty minute mark most of Ms. Daly's students were on their feet shouting invective at their guest.

Ms. Daly grew increasingly fearful that her friend Harris would be physically attacked. She sought to stem the tide of anger by hurrying to the front of the room and screaming at her students.

Harris exhibited no sign of concern. He removed his head gear and his *thawb*. He smiled at the students. He shouted to the class, "It's only an act."

Gradually the students began to quiet. Ms. Daly introduced the guest as Mr. Harris, a former New York actor. She complimented him on his realistic portrayal of a jihadist. She asked the students to applaud Mr. Harris's performance. A few did but quite reluctantly.

Mr. Harris left the room, uninjured.

By the next morning phone calls nearly overwhelmed Principal David Kenwick's line. About sixty-five percent demanded that Ms. Daly be fired immediately. No patriotic American should ever be exposed to such insidious propaganda.

The other thirty-five percent expressed approval of Ms. Daly's use of a role player.

Most of the students when asked their opinion laughed ruefully and admitted that while they had been thoroughly taken in they had learned much more about jihadists and their rationale for their terrorist activities.

They said, too, that they now better understood the danger that such groups as al Qaeda and ISIS present to America.

One particularly patriotic senior proclaimed his love for America and his intention to "join up" at the end of his senior year to fight jihadists.

Liz Daly complimented him on his patriotism. However, the incident upset her for some time.

At last she decided she had done the right thing.

TEN
Mr. Martin's Titles

Mr. Gaspar Martin taught French in an inner city public high school. A Canadian from Quebec, Mr. Martin had grown up in a very formal family. Both his father and mother taught in an upscale private school, the school he had attended in his teens; thus he came to the United States and his teaching assignment in the inner city with a strong sense of proper behavior.

On the first day of class he instructed his students to always call him *Mr.* Martin. Never were they to call him anything else—in school, at home, nowhere, never. In turn he would always address them as Mr. or Miss in class. Instead of LaVonra, his first name to his mother, and Gator to his friends, the student LaVonra Breshears became *Mr.* Breshears. Instead of Sipliah, first name to her mother and every teacher in the school, and Sippy to her friends, Sipliah Hawkins became *Miss* Hawkins. And so it went.

All of which went quite well. The students rather liked being recognized as Mr. or Miss. And they reciprocated when called upon in class by rising to stand beside their desks, clearing their throats, and saying, "Mr. Martin, Miss Hawkins (or whomever) requests permission to speak." And Martin in turn would say, "Permission to speak is granted, Miss Hawkins." All very formal.

Then one afternoon as Mr. Martin cut across the back of the auditorium, a shortcut from his room to the teachers' lounge, he chanced to overhear the words of three members of his French class. Seated at a table on stage as they waited for rehearsal to begin for a play in which they had roles, they were evaluating his class—and him. One of them, Mr. Gholson, said, "Well, you know, Gassy can't help himself; after all, he's a frog (a derogatory term for Frenchmen)." Giggles. Agreement.

Mr. Martin stepped from backstage and up to the table, thereby surprising the holy goo out of his students. He said only one thing. "Gassy the Frog heard that." He turned and walked away.

Nothing more was said about the incident until mid-term grades came out. Mr. Gholson, Miss Tenley, and Miss Curry each received C-plus as a grade. That caused a great outcry from all three of the students. All believed they had earned B-pluses or even A's. After class the three trooped en masse to Mr. Martin's desk and protested their grades.

Mr. Martin looked up, smiled a sardonic sort of smile, and said, "You all know why Gassy the Frog lowered your marks slightly." He turned back to the book he was reading. The three students yelped and hollered and pleaded, but Mr. Martin did not even acknowledge that he heard them.

Of course the brouhaha did not end there. Bright and early the next morning the mothers of all three "victims" charged into the principal's office demanding justice. Ms. Lufkin, the principal, who had known nothing about the grade matter previously, recognized that she had a problem.

THE DILEMMA

On the one hand Ms. Lufkin knew how much Mr. Martin held to his belief that a teacher should be respected and honored and whatever decisions he made about his students, including the grades he gave them, should be inviolate, final. She knew he would resist any grade change.

On the other hand, the three mothers were not going to be easily placated—not at all—unless their children's grades were changed. Indeed, Ms. Lufkin could see the matter going first to the school board, and then, were the matter still not settled to the satisfaction of the parents, to the courts.

Before she did anything else, Ms. Lufkin excused herself for a moment from the presence of the three women, went into a separate conference room, took a sheet of paper and jotted down a few words, the most salient being a question, "Should I support Mr. Martin?"

THE DEBATE

Pro

Yes, by all means Ms. Lufkin should support Mr. Martin. She should support all her teachers, especially with regard to grades that are given. If she does not, she will have a faculty revolt on her hands far worse than anything the students' parents can bring.

One of the biggest and most dangerous problems with today's public schools is the lack of respect for the authority of teachers. Even into the 1970s respect for teachers was a given. Teachers were masters of their classrooms. Now that respect not only for teachers, but also for people in general, seems to have largely perished.

Mr. Martin sought to impress upon his students that respect for others is important. Alas and alack, these days he may be fighting a losing battle. Even the president of the United States is heckled when he speaks.

Unfortunately many teachers contribute vastly to the lack of respect they receive from their students. They permit students to call them by their first names in class. They dress informally. They attempt to pal with the students.

Mr. Martin represents a time in the past when students and parents recognized that education is a serious undertaking, that it is not fun and games but rather important work, hard work, necessary work if the nation is to survive. And the teacher is to be respected and not called by derogatory names.

The grade assigned is the grade received.

Ms. Lufkin should know that. She should support Mr. Martin fully.

We need far more Mr. Martins in the classrooms of America.

Con

No, Ms. Lufkin should *not* support Mr. Martin.

If idle gossip among students about their teachers outside class were grounds for lowering their grades, few students would ever get a passing grade. Students always discuss their teachers and often in unflattering terms. Most of such talk is quite harmless. Too, it is most likely that the majority of the students in Mr. Martin's French class outside of class in their private conversations referred to him as "Gassy," and/or "a frog," not merely the three whose grades he lowered.

A similar case: in the days before shaved heads and total baldness were common, a school in Florida employed a science teacher who through some type of affliction had not a single hair on his head. His students called him "Chrome Dome." After he learned of his nickname, he instructed each of his classes that while he had no objection to their use of "Chrome Dome," outside class, he forbade the moniker to be used within his earshot. Otherwise, he joked in a pseudo threatening way, "If you do use that name and I hear you, I'll have to slap you up 'long side the head." A very good and sensible approach to the matter, one Mr. Martin should emulate.

If Mr. Martin continues to be as unbending as he appears to be, he probably should be let go at the end of the semester. He does not possess the temperament of a successful teacher.

Chapter 10

THE RESOLUTION

Ms. Lufkin returned to her office and sent a secretary to fetch Mr. Martin.

After being verbally assaulted for five minutes or so, Mr. Martin explained that he had overheard their reference to his first name and the frog business, and therefore he had docked their grades. The mothers did not accept his explanation, not at all. Neither, really, did Ms. Lufkin.

Quietly she asked Mr. Martin to change the students' grades to the grade they had earned through their classroom work. For a half hour or so Mr. Martin resisted the pleas and threats, but at last, the three parents and Ms. Lufkin having worn him down, he agreed to a mild compromise. He would change the miscreants' grades to B's.

While the mothers initially rejected the compromise, still holding out for "the real grades," at last they, too, by then themselves worn down, very reluctantly agreed to the B grade, and left the principal's office, still muttering imprecations.

Ms. Gholson returned to Ms. Lufkin's office long enough to warn her that Mr. Martin should be terminated at the end of the school year.

"Or else!"

ELEVEN

To Run? Not to Run?

Ms. Marlene Bonner, who taught civics in a California high school with just more than twelve hundred enrollment, enjoyed great popularity among her students. They found her classes interesting. They found her exciting, passionate about her subject, and inspirational. Her students soon came to believe that American democracy depended on citizen participation in the process of government.

Thus when the city was to hold a city council election three of Ms. Bonner's students, Frank Johnson, Luis Lopez, and Mark Belson, approached her to ask a question: "Did she really believe what she taught?"

Puzzled, Ms. Bonner answered that of course she believed what she taught.

"Okay," said Luis Lopez, "then you really do believe that American citizens have an obligation to be informed about government and to participate in it?"

Ms. Bonner sensed she was being set up. "Yes, I believe that."

Frank Johnson said, "We want you to run for city council."

Ms. Bonner laughed. "Oh, no. You don't mean it, do you?"

They did mean it. They presented her with several sheets of petitions asking her to declare herself a candidate for city council. Eight hundred and forty-eight high school students had signed the petitions.

THE DILEMMA

Marlene Bonner considered the matter. Definitely her students wanted her to run, a great tribute to her, she realized. How could she turn them down? They believed in her; they believed in citizen participation in government. If she refused to run, would some become cynical about what she had taught them? Would they believe she did not *really* believe in a citizen's duty to participate?

Still, she wondered, might it not be an ethics violation for a teacher, herself, to run for public office in the city where she taught civics? Even though the students who had signed the petitions were not old enough to vote, possibly they could influence the votes of those who were old enough like their parents and others. She realized that if she did run her opponents would scream to the heavens that she had a conflict of interest because she could influence voters, if in no other way, they would charge, by threatening the grades of her students.

Should she run? She considered the matter carefully.

THE DEBATE

Pro

Yes, Ms. Bonner definitely should run for a city council seat. What better way to prove to the youth she taught that she truly believed that all citizens in a democracy have the right and, indeed, the obligation to participate in decisions made about their governance.

One of the biggest problems of today's political system is that too few highly intelligent and eminently qualified citizens are willing to stand for election. The coarseness and the vitriol of the campaigns, the mud slinging, the unfounded half-truths and actual lies about the candidates warn off many good people who are unwilling to be exposed to such slime.

What a great learning experience for young people to have their teacher offer herself to the voters! Would America had many more citizens like her!

Con

Can anyone say "partisan"? A teacher who teaches civics to high school students should not be running for political office, at least not in her own community.

One of the oft-heard complaints made by conservatives about college professors is that they are overwhelmingly liberal and spread their liberal views through virtual indoctrination of their students. Ms. Bonner is not a college teacher, but a variant of the same criticism applies.

Thus the question must be addressed: will Ms. Bonner skew the minds of her students toward her candidacy by what she says in class? How can her students fairly examine and evaluate the positions of her opponents? They cannot.

Another valid argument against her running is the matter of time. How can she find the time to campaign if she is attending properly to her teaching duties?

If Ms. Bonner runs for the city council seat, she should resign her teaching position before declaring her candidacy.

THE RESOLUTION

Feeling that she could not disappoint her students and former students, Marlene Bonner did run for a city council seat. She agreed to run only if the students who urged her candidacy ran her campaign. And they did. Frank Johnson served as campaign manager, Luis Lopez as treasurer, and Mark Belson as publicist.

Although none of her five opponents gave Ms. Bonner much of a chance, they did take out ads attacking her—half-truths and downright lying ads, charging her with using school supplies to get her message out, speculating about why she had never married, hinting that she favored black kids over white kids in her classes.

Some days Ms. Bonner wished she had never entered the race, but she did what she had taught her students to do: smile and persist; never give up.

With two seats to be filled, on the night of the election the city's residents were surprised to learn that Ms. Marlene Bonner had come within one hundred and two votes of becoming a city council member, having finished third among the candidates.

Knowing a candidate's supporters always required an election night party, Ms. Bonner, who coached girls' basketball in addition to her classroom duties, lined up the school gym and her volunteers came in to play basketball.

When the results of the election came in, she stepped up on the third row of the bleachers, looked at the expectant faces of her students, and said, "I'm *so* proud of all of you. You've made such a difference."

Then she choked back tears as she managed one more sentence. "Whose ball is it?"

TWELVE

The Absentees

Alvin Swanson taught small business management classes for seniors in a Kansas high school. Each semester he required his students to research a small business of their choice and toward the end of the class deliver an oral presentation about the business, how it started, why it was successful—or wasn't—its management practices, that sort of thing. At the beginning of the semester Swanson okayed or rejected the students' proposals as to what business they chose to research.

Enrolled in a spring semester class were two boys, Early Null, an all-conference catcher on the high school baseball team, and Howard Latimer, a heavy metal band musician.

In February Null approached Mr. Swanson to ask if he might miss a week of classes in March. The St. Louis Cardinals baseball team had a tryout camp scheduled for that week, it being the spring break time for most college players who would be attending the camp. Null's high school had no spring break. He would miss a week of school.

However, Null had another problem. The business he planned to visit for his class project, a business called Swift Snaps, a manufacturer of clothing featuring snap closings, had scheduled his visit for the same day the tryout camp began. Could he change to another business?

Mr. Swanson said he would decide soon and let Null know his decision.

But before Mr. Swanson got back to Null with an okay or a no, Howard Latimer came to request a day's leave of absence to travel to Dallas to pay a last visit to his grandmother who was dying of cancer. Howard also wondered if he might change business projects, his original choice called Whoompers, a sound system business, having gone out of business.

Mr. Swanson approved both absences.

Null's absence week passed, five days of class missed.

Latimer, who was expected to return on Monday, having missed class the previous Friday, did not appear. Not until the following Monday did he come back to class. Six class meetings missed. His grandmother had lingered. He had stayed for a long good-bye.

Null gave his oral report on the tryout camp, in his opinion certainly a business enterprise. His student audience liked his report.

Latimer gave his report on the new business he had chosen, Meow and Moo, a company that produced animal toys and books for preschool children. Latimer made his report amusing but relevant to the requirements laid out by Swanson at the beginning of the semester. The students *loved* his report.

THE DILEMMA

At the end of the semester when final grades were to be recorded, Swanson found that when he averaged the marks for Early Null and Howard Latimer, they both averaged out to ninety-three points, if a point more an A, if a point less, an A-minus.

Swanson thought more. Both had given excellent end-of-semester reports on their business projects. Null had missed five days of class. For a baseball tryout camp.

Latimer had missed six days, five days more than he had said he would miss. But to say good-bye to his grandmother. Hmmm.

Should he give Null the higher grade, an A, and Latimer the lower grade, an A-minus? Hmmm.

THE DEBATE

Pro

Yes, Mr. Swanson should give Null the higher grade and Latimer one lower. It is probable that Latimer missed class to go to Dallas for reasons that had nothing or little to do with his grandmother's medical condition. Latimer presented no evidence of his actual whereabouts, no obituary or hospital notice, nothing like that, when he returned to class. And he had been gone five days beyond what he had requested.

The real question is: is anything of value learned from attending class? Most teachers agree that class attendance has value. Of course. Otherwise why attend class at all?

No, Mr. Swanson is perfectly justified in giving Latimer a lower grade.

Con

It is possible that Latimer did lie about his grandmother being at death's door, but how would Swanson have known that? He did not insist that Latimer bring back a certified copy of her death notice.

In truth, a better guess than why Latimer returned late is a guess about why Swanson favored Null with the higher grade. A good guess might be that Swanson, quite likely a baseball fan, possibly a Cardinals fan, let that influence the grade just a little.

Remember, too, the subject businesses of the two youths' reports. Null reported about his experiences at the tryout camp. Really? A business? Perhaps a case can be made that it was a minor branch of the St. Louis Cardinals' total enterprise, but that is all.

However, compare Latimer's report with Null's. Latimer reported on a real business; moreover, the students enjoyed his report more. Shouldn't the students' reception of a classmate's work be a factor in grading?

THE RESOLUTION

A week after the grades went out, school still in session for underclassmen, the seniors released from classes, Swanson received a notice from the school's Judiciary Council, a student tribunal set up to permit students to lodge complaints over real or imagined slights.

Mr. Swanson was charged with discrimination by Howard Latimer, citing Early Null's grade of A being undeserved inasmuch as his grade with the exact numerical average as Null received only an A-minus.

At the meeting of the Judiciary Council Swanson attempted to justify his grade discrimination with a recounting of the absence story.

Latimer presented his evidence in the manner of an experienced attorney, contending that Swanson, being a baseball fan, had favored Null.

After the presentation of evidence, the Judiciary Council met, having decided that Latimer's A-minus should be changed to an A.

Thoroughly disgusted, Swanson changed Latimer's grade.

Ten months later Swanson read Latimer's grandmother's obituary, carried in the local paper because she had lived locally before moving to Dallas.

THIRTEEN
Patty v. the Bully

Mildred Downing taught science classes at Edward McNair Middle School for forty-one years. In her last semester before retirement she had observed that a boy from another class regularly bullied one of her students during lunch breaks and after school.

The girl, Patty, was obese, weighing close to one-hundred and seventy pounds. Moreover, she was very quiet and a bit slow mentally.

The bully, a sixth grader named Arlen Royce, was called Hup by friends and foes alike because of his routine of circling his victims as he crouched and called out, "Hup, hup, hup" as a kind of signal that he meant to psychologically and sometimes physically assail them. He chose his victims carefully, never picking on boys bigger than he.

Arlen often chose girls as his victims, especially if they wore glasses, were unusually tall or short, came from a poor family, or simply were not part of the "snotty girls" clique.

Ms. Downing's student Patty qualified on all counts. Additionally she had a noticeable speech impediment, and her father worked on a garbage truck. An eminently excellent candidate to be bullied.

Ms. Downing not only knew of the bullying, she knew, too, that Arlen was punished very little when sent to the principal's office. She guessed the mild penalties might have something to do with the fact that Arlen's father was the city's mayor.

Ms. Downing felt great sympathy for Patty and wanted to help her. But how?

Now, in the last month of her teaching career, she had an idea. But . . .

Chapter 13

THE DILEMMA

Ms. Downing's idea was quite simple. Have Patty attack Arlen when he tried to bully her. After all, Patty outweighed Arlen by fifty pounds and was several inches taller. Moreover, the fact that Patty was female improved the plan immeasurably ... if it succeeded.

Ms. Downing realized that so much could go wrong with her plan. First of all, it might never get off the ground. Patty might not agree to it, and even if she did she might not be able to handle Arlen.

Too, Ms. Downing considered, what risk was there to her if the plan was carried out successfully? Would she be opening herself to litigation?

Yet, she felt she must do *something* to improve Patty's already-bottomed-out self-esteem.

For two weeks Ms. Downing wrestled with the wisdom of her plan. She told her husband about it and asked his advice. He laughed and told her, "Go for it."

She just didn't know.

Should she encourage Patty to physically attack Arlen?

THE DEBATE

Pro

Yes, she should. She is right; she must do something to help Patty. If she doesn't, the poor girl will have no future. Arlen will continue to bully her all the way through high school. Indeed, he is likely to step up his efforts at intimidation.

Ms. Downing is probably correct in her belief that Patty can physically overpower Arlen. She is bigger. There is little difference in the strength of boys and girls before puberty. Moreover, Patty will have the advantage of surprise. Arlen will not expect her to defend herself, let alone assail him.

If Patty does attack Arlen when he next attempts to bully her, and if her attack is successful by any measure, she will gain much greater self-confidence. When Arlen attempts to bully her again, she will simply laugh at him.

Too, if she launches a successful attack she will gain considerable "cred" with her classmates, many of whom no doubt dislike his bullying ways but have, like Patty, been intimidated by him. With an attack's good outcome most of them will embrace Patty for her defense of herself, and, indirectly, her defense of them.

Ms. Downing is concerned about the possibility of Arlen's parents or other parents learning that she really instigated the attack and that knowledge resulting in a suit of some sort.

Such a suit would go nowhere given Mr. Downing's excellent reputation as a beloved teacher over a long, long time. It is probably a safe wager that several of the present school board members have been Ms. Downing's students in years back.

As Ms. Downing's husband advised: "Go for it!"

Con

Ms. Downing may have been in the classroom for forty-one years, but it is obvious she understands little about the perils of educators exposing themselves to risks these days. For starters if it is learned that she "sicced" Patty on Arlen, she will be sued either by Arlen's parents or Patty's parents or both. Suppose one of the pupils involved is injured. It will be charged that Ms. Downing did not supervise her students, almost a capital offense these days.

Beyond the risk of litigation, the idea that this exercise will halt Arlen's bullying habits is doubtful. Indeed, the exercise may cause Arlen to become *more* aggressive, perhaps to the point of doing something very serious. He will seek revenge, thereby putting Patty in jeopardy of greater harm.

What should Ms. Downing do? The answer is easy: nothing. Probably little can be done by classroom teachers to curb Arlen. Bullies who are bullies in middle school seldom change. They remain bullies all through high school and into adulthood. They are the athletes who intimidate teammates and foes alike. They are the husbands who beat their wives. And if they climb up the corporate ladder, they are the demanding bosses hated by their employees.

The boy or girl who shows a bullying propensity in preschool or in the first three grades can be corrected to become more of a "plays-well-with-others" child. After the bully gets older by his or her ninth or tenth year the only way to break the bullying habit is for his/her classmates to view his actions disdainfully or to ignore him.

No, Ms. Downing, you are about to retire so leave well enough alone. Take no action.

THE RESOLUTION

On a Tuesday morning Ms. Downing found Patty and spoke to her privately. She instructed the girl on what she must do. At first Patty was reluctant to do what her teacher suggested. But Ms. Downing persisted, explaining to Patty that it was now or never. Five more years of Arlen, eighth grade through senior high—would she want that? Patty must stop the bullying now.

After lunch when the students were returning to class, several lined up in the hall to get a drink at the water fountain. Sensing this could be the time the plan might be implemented, Ms. Downing stayed in her room rather than accompanying the children into the hall. She closed the door to the hall slightly, leaving enough gap between the door and the wall to let her see what happened if Arlen appeared as he frequently did at that time of day.

Sure enough, as if on cue, Arlen came swaggering down the hall. He paused at the water fountain.

As planned Patty managed to position herself in the water line directly behind Arlen. As Ms. Downing peeked through the door-wall gap, she saw Patty reach forward with a forefinger and thump Arlen solidly on his shoulder. The thump surprised Arlen. He looked around. He saw Patty grinning at him. He immediately cleared the space ahead of him and behind Patty. He went into his trademarked attack posture, circling Patty as he crouched, moving his hands in a "come and get me" manner, chanting his "hup, hup, hup," and snarling, "Fat Pat the ugly cat."

In the past when Arlen had tormented Patty, she had stood stock still and sobbed as he circled her, but this time she moved *toward* him. Her unexpected move caused him to stop for a second or two to assess the situation. Too late. She swung her fist. Instinctively he brought his arm up to block her punch. A mistake. Because his arm caused her fist to divert in direction, not continuing in its intended path to his chin, but causing her arm to circle around Arlen's shoulder. Attempting to rid himself of this hideous configuration, Arlen swatted at the offending arm causing him to lose his balance and likewise causing Patty to lose her balance.

Arlen toppled over onto his back. Patty toppled over squarely on top of him, pinning him under her. He screamed at her to "get off!" Patty would have been only too glad to "get off," but her horizontal position and the fact that Arlen had, again instinctively, clutched her ample body as he had fallen prevented Patty from doing anything but remaining just as she was.

The novel sight of Patty, the intended victim, smothering Arlen, the intended bully, caused their classmates to react in different ways. While a few girls gasped and clasped their hands to their mouths, most of the other students laughed, some uproariously, and some even gibed Arlen, pointing their fingers toward him and hollering insults.

After waiting a few seconds to give the situation time to impress itself on the minds of the students, Ms. Downing stepped out of the classroom and restored order.

As she lifted herself off Arlen's body, Patty turned her head toward the teacher and smiled slightly.

FOURTEEN

Love in the Classroom

Two weeks before she taught her first class in a small Kansas high school, rookie teacher Diane Bellows moved to the tiny house her parents had rented for her. The house owner had wanted it occupied all the time, even before school started.

Knowing no one in the town and lonely, one week after her move Diane walked the short distance from her house to a downtown fast food place to eat her evening meal. She ordered a cheeseburger and took a seat in a booth.

A tall, handsome young man came in, ordered, turned to her, and asked if he might join her.

She motioned him to the seat opposite her. She introduced herself and explained she was the new English teacher at the high school. It was, she said, her first teaching job out of college.

He was Andy Wyman. He ran a computer repair service.

They talked and found they had several common interests—in music, the movies, actors, and more. They laughed with each other.

She liked him. He offered to drive her back to her house. She accepted.

On her first day of teaching, Diane Bellows gasped when into her fifth period senior English class walked Andy Wyman.

After class she stopped him and asked why he had not told her that he was a high school student when they had first met. He apologized, smiled, and agreed he should have told her. But—he shrugged—he had enjoyed their visit in the restaurant so much he had "forgotten to tell her."

He said he might seem older than the other students because he was. A serious illness had caused him to miss a year of school when he was seven years old. He was now eighteen, nearly nineteen.

He left the classroom. Luckily she had a free period before her last class of the day. She spent most of her free period composing herself. Dammit anyway! She liked him, she knew that, but *loved* him? How could she love him? They had talked only that first time at the fast food place.

For two weeks Diane managed to keep her emotions in check during the senior English class. Andy spoke to her only during class, but through discreet inquiry she learned more about him. A farm boy, he was an only child. He played quarterback on the high school team.

She learned one more thing: for two years he had gone steady with a cheerleader named Marta, one of Diane's students in the junior class. That romance had ended when Marta fell hard for a new boy in school, another junior named Cappy.

At the end of the second week just as Diane was closing her teacher's text, the door to her classroom opened and Andy Wyman entered. She sucked in her breath and greeted him. "Hi, what are you doing?"

He talked to her first about the football game that night and asked if she would be there. She said she would. Presently he moved the conversation to talk about a movie playing Saturday night in the nearby larger city. "Would you like to go?" he asked. "With me, I mean."

She affected an alas-alack expression. "I'd like to but, of course, we can't. You know that."

"I know," he agreed. "Students can't date teachers, but if no one knew." He outlined his plan to keep their date secret.

She listened. Then, her heart overcoming her head's resistance, she agreed to meet him in a small, out-of-the-way café in the city.

They fell in love.

He was four years younger than she, but why should that matter, she asked herself. Age differences in marriage partners were common.

After their dates, she always came back to the harsh reality that if the school board even found out she was dating a student, she would be summarily dismissed. She knew it.

They were careful about their trysts, always waiting two weeks between dates, never hinting of their secret in class, sitting in the back of the theater when they went to the movies.

In April the five school board members met to discuss teacher contracts for the coming year. All went quite smoothly until they came to Diane Bellows. Yes, she was an excellent teacher; the kids liked her.

Then a board member, a minister named Taylor Creedling, the pastor of a non-denominational church which counted some parishioners from the nearby city, cleared his throat and confessed he must tell what he knew about Diane Bellows. It turned out that the owner of a small café in the city, a member of Creedling's church, had seen the football player Wyman there several times with the English teacher Bellows.

THE DILEMMA

Should they, must they, dismiss Ms. Bellows immediately?

The other board members demanded to know how long Creedling had known of this matter. He admitted he had known for several months. He apologized for not telling the others.

"God, yes, you should have told us," sputtered board member Stan Barstow. "We can't have a teacher dating a student. There's stuff in the paper about that all the time, teachers seducing students. Not only is the teacher fired, but sometimes she goes to prison. Why in the hell didn't you tell us?"

The Reverend Creedling cleared his throat again. "Well, the Sunday when I was told about this was the Sunday before the state championship football game the next Saturday. The game where Wyman passed for three touchdowns and ran for two more."

"Oh," squeaked Stan Barstow. The other board members sat similarly transfixed before a member named Kauffman asked quietly, "Do you think they're married?"

The Reverend Creedling did not know.

A fourth board member, the town librarian, Eloise Michelson, said softly, "The students really like Miss Bellows. They think she's the best English teacher they've ever had."

The discussion of Ms. Bellows's future continued until at last Kauffman said, "All right, we can't argue all night. Should she be terminated?"

THE DEBATE

Pro

Of course Ms. Bellows should be terminated immediately. There cannot be any sort of relationship between teacher and student such as that between Ms. Bellows and Andy Wyman. The Reverend Creedling should have blown the whistle as soon as he knew about the teacher-student relationship. It is clear, of course, why the reverend kept the secret. To have "spilled the beans" before the state football championship might have distracted the star Andy Wyman from his focus on winning the game.

The librarian's report that students liked Ms. Bellows is entirely beside the point.

Teachers who are seducing students are frequently quite charismatic and well liked by other students. That is exactly why such teachers are dangerous.

Further, we don't know that Ms. Bellows did not give undeserved grades to Andy Wyman. She might have. We don't know that she did not.

In short, the board of education should dismiss Ms. Bellows immediately, tomorrow, not the next day. Certainly they should not consider retaining her in their school for the next year.

Con

First of all, the grades Ms. Bellows gave Andy Wyman are quite consistent with the grades given him in his other classes. Clearly he is a superior student with a high degree of intellect.

Second, she is not guilty of seducing a student who is under the age of consent. Andy is not sixteen or younger. Were the romance between a young man eighteen years old and a young woman twenty-two years old, just people, not student and teacher, none of us would find anything wrong with that.

Third, Diane and Andy were very circumspect with their relationship. They understood their love, if known, would be misinterpreted and damaged by gossip by holier-than-thou goodie two-shoes. And, yes, of course, they understood full well she would be fired forthwith. By being extraordinarily cautious they showed they cared about not only each other, but also others.

And last, consider the upshot had Reverend Creedling run through the streets of their small town proclaiming the news that star quarterback Andy Wyman was dating English teacher Diane Bellows. The town would have been torn asunder with cries that Bellows must be dismissed set against demands that Wyman, no matter his involvement, must be permitted to play in the championship game.

THE RESOLUTION

It was late April when the school board discussed this matter, less than a month before the end of the school year. After much discussion Reverend Creedling was detailed to visit with the miscreant couple to tell them that the romance was known about by the board members, but no one else.

The Reverend asked them not to date again until the school year had ended, until Andy had graduated. Then they could date openly if they wished.

In June Diane and Andy were married.

FIFTEEN
Santa or Satan

Rufus Shay, in 1972 an English teacher at Vanders High School, knew of the Twerp Club, or TCs, the students' designation for a group of ten or eleven ninth-grade boys who hung out together. None of the TCs participated in any sports. They often went to the school library after the day's classes to work on lessons.

The TCs liked the librarian, one Alton Yelson, who helped them find materials they needed, suggested approaches they might take in writing their essays, and gave advice about how they might respond to bullying. The TCs were subject to considerable bullying.

While Rufus Shay believed Alton Yelson to be gay (though he had never "come out"), he also believed no one can choose his or her sexual orientation—that it is what it is. Nor did he think it mattered much. Alton did his job as librarian very well. And he saw no evidence that Alton ever sought to change anyone else's sexual preferences.

Rufus felt a certain sympathy for Alton, a man largely ignored by other faculty members. Thus Rufus made it a point to visit with Alton nearly every day. Soon it was apparent to Rufus that Alton considered him a good friend, really the only true friend he had on the faculty.

Two faculty members, Charley Kranz and Ramon Hemjy, began to take particular note of the TC boys' afternoon visits to the library. In the teachers' lounge during their free periods Charley and Ramon talked about the "situation" more and more. They were certain that Alton planned to "put a move on" one or more of the TCs. By November they spoke of the need to alert parents of the boys involved that their sons were in danger of being seduced by, in Charley's words, "an out-and-out queer."

Charley and Ramon's discussions disgusted Rufus, especially when he happened to overhear the two speculating about his own sexual orientation They pointed out to a third teacher that "Rufus spends a lot of time with Alton." Angered by the innuendo, Rufus said nothing but quit going to the teachers' lounge.

On the first Saturday in December Alton invited the TCs to his apartment for a pre-Christmas party. He made popcorn balls, gave each a soft drink, and favored each with a small knife as a present. When the boys went home they told their parents about the party. They had had a good time.

Nothing to be alarmed about. Nine of the ten parents saw it that way, but not the tenth parent, a carpenter named Tony Fellsmere. He had heard about Alton. His neighbor, the teacher Charley Kranz, had warned him. Alton meant to have "weird sex" with those boys.

Tony Fellsmere demanded something be done. Charley Kranz said he would look into the matter.

On Monday Charley ordered Rufus to come to the teachers' lounge during his free period. There with Ramon present, Charley told Rufus of his "great concern."

"Think how it will harm the whole teaching profession if this stuff gets out," said Charley. "You're his friend, Rufus. We've got to know more about 'our fairy librarian.' You're his friend."

While Rufus thought his fellow faculty members' suspicions were ridiculous, he asked what Charley and Ramon thought he should or could do.

Charley answered, "Find out more about him. He's been here three years. Where was he before? Why did he leave? Make some discreet inquiries." He added, "If he's a 'queer' and has it in his head to molest the boys, we've got to stop it. We've got to."

Reluctantly, Rufus agreed to learn more about Alton's past.

Rufus remembered that Alton had once told him that he "was in therapy." He had explained little more about it; nor had Rufus asked.

THE DILEMMA

Rufus thought of various means by which he might get further information about Alton, the sort of information Charley wanted.

He thought about concocting a story about a friend who needed therapy to cope with battlefield stress from Vietnam. Perhaps Alton would reveal the name of his therapist, and he, Rufus, could then question the therapist. But would a therapist tell him anything about a patient? Wasn't such information confidential?

In the next minutes Rufus berated himself for even thinking about such deception. My god! What a terrible way to treat a friend. And Alton was his friend.

Yet, on the other hand, suppose Alton *was* meaning to lure one or more of the TC boys into some kind of unsavory and perhaps dangerous relationship.

Rufus wrestled with the matter for several days.

Should he attempt to pry very personal information out of a fellow teacher?

THE DEBATE

Pro

Yes, this is a case of possibly preventing a crime before it occurs rather than doing nothing although you know it can occur and most likely will occur. If he can, Rufus should learn the name and address of the therapist treating Alton Yelson. With this information Rufus can contact the therapist and tell him of the situation. If in the opinion of the therapist there is no danger that the librarian is bent on the seduction of young boys, then Rufus can simply report to Charley and Ramon that there is no danger, and the matter can be put to rest.

If, on the other hand, the therapist does see a possible danger, while his files are quite properly confidential, he may be able to alert the proper school administrators, perhaps the principal and/or school board members to the danger present and action may be taken to forestall anything untoward or criminal from occurring.

Because this does involve children, it is very important that Rufus make this effort.

Con

What insanity! What crime has Alton committed? He invited several boys whom he knew were bullied and needed boosts to their self-esteem over to his home to share a bit of Christmas cheer with him. What is wrong with that? Football coaches, basketball coaches, do exactly what Alton did all the time—have players in their homes, give them soft drinks and cookies. No one believes that constitutes a threat of moral turpitude.

Rufus would be using exceedingly poor judgment if he were to betray Alton's friendship by concocting a fictional tale about a "friend" needing a therapist. He should simply ignore the gossip of Charley and Ramon. If he does, the likelihood is that Alton will remain the librarian, the TC boys will continue to frequent the library, a laudable activity, and the school year will move along smoothly.

If Rufus does do what Charley and Ramon suggest, and he finds nothing criminal or at all morally reprehensible in Alton's past, and Alton learns of all this, he might possibly sue the teachers involved as well as the school for defamation of character.

Alton may well be awarded thousands or even millions of dollars. And justly so.

No, Rufus, do *not* pry into Alton's private world, not without much more evidence than merely invidious gossip and supposition from two fellow teachers.

THE RESOLUTION

After vacillating for a week, Rufus decided to lie. He reported to Charley and Ramon that he had met with Alton's therapist who affirmed that the librarian represented no danger to anyone. Rufus resisted saying more, telling the other two teachers that what he had learned he had promised to keep confidential. Neither did he vouchsafe any information about the therapist—who existed only in Rufus's mind.

Neither of the two teachers involved, Charley or Ramon, was retained by the district for the next year. Alton continued in the library. The TC boys moved on to their high school years before going on to college.

For years Rufus continued to play the matter over in his mind, wondering if he had done the right thing.

SIXTEEN
No News Is Good News

Blythe Calhoun taught art classes at Percy Loggins High School. She was well liked by her students even though they thought her classes quite demanding and intense. When the bell rang dismissing students from their previous classes, she stood at her classroom door urging them to hurry in, go to their art lockers, get the supplies needed for the class, get to their seats, and be ready to go.

Over the sixteen years she had taught the class Blythe had complained about many things but constantly about one thing—the length of the class period. She insisted that little could be done in the forty-seven minutes allotted. Her fledgling Rembrandts could hardly be expected to fully develop their talents in so short a time.

Indeed, her complaints paid off. Before her eighth year of nagging, the school board approved a rearrangement of the class schedule so that two back-to-back periods were available to her serious art students.

This rearrangement placated Blythe until the *Youth News* program was put on the school's TV sets at ten a.m., the beginning time for Blythe's double period class.

Youth News was exactly what the name implied, a fifteen-minute news program aimed at high school students. Thousands of high schools across America ran the program daily

The administration at Percy Loggins decreed that every classroom in the school would show *Youth News*, the reasoning being that teenagers need to pay more attention to "serious" happenings nationally and across the world.

Blythe Calhoun resented the program's intrusion into her artists' time. Sure she would be ordered to air the program if she complained to the principal, she simply ignored the decree that *Youth News* be aired. If asked about it, she would say she must have missed seeing the edict.

That strategy worked for three weeks until the principal happened to stop by her classroom one morning while *Youth News* was supposed to be airing. He called her into his office after school, dressed her down a bit, and told her she *must* show the program. He threatened major repercussions if she continued to ignore his order.

THE DILEMMA

After her meeting with the principal, Blythe considered her options. If she obeyed the principal's directive, she would lose fifteen minutes of precious work time every day, actually more than fifteen minutes because time would be lost while the students got their supplies and started work.

But, she thought, if she turned on the TV with the sound muted she could tell her students to get their materials and once they were seated she could then instruct them in art. They could simply ignore *Youth News*. And if anyone asked if she ran the news program in her classroom, she could truthfully answer that yes, she had the TV on.

Yet, of course, she recognized that while she might technically be following the principal's orders, her "cuteness" would anger him. He might then really "do something."

Blythe's dilemma: should she comply with the decree or not?

THE DEBATE

Pro

Of course she should have her students watch *Youth News*. For several reasons.

First, because high school students know far too little about national and world events. *Youth News* provides important news in a form palatable to teenagers.

Second, Blythe's students are fully aware that they are supposed to watch *Youth News* every morning and pay attention to it, not merely have it on the TV set as they do other things. Their teacher's flouting the rules sets a bad example for them.

Third, if the principal becomes sufficiently angry when he learns that Blythe has circumvented his order, he may make life quite unpleasant for her.

The only sensible thing Blythe can—and *must*—do is to have her students seated at their desks quietly watching *Youth News*.

Con

In the first place the order that every student in the building must watch *Youth News*, whether the order comes from the principal or the school board, is useless and even a bit silly.

Blythe's class will not be the only class largely ignoring the program as it runs. In other classes in the school students will be visiting with each other. Some will be completing homework. Some will be looking over the crop of opposite-sex students in the room. Some will be merely daydreaming.

Youth News is a commercially sponsored program with items advertised which may or may not be in the students' best interest to consume, food and drinks particularly. Schools are at fault for permitting such programs in the classrooms.

Finally, why should a teacher not be the one who decides what goes on in the classroom so long as it is in keeping with the basic subject matter? Why should Blythe sacrifice time working on the subject about which she is so passionate—art—to world and national news, a topic better left to the civics and history teachers in the school? No doubt many leading figures in a whole variety of disciplines have little knowledge of the "news," and they do not need to have it in order to live a full and happy life.

While Blythe may be forced to have her students watch the news program, it is an entirely unreasonable requirement.

THE RESOLUTION

Blythe thought briefly about leaving Percy Loggins High School, but given the circumstances of her life—her students whom she did not want to abandon, her friends on the faculty and in the community, her husband's job, all that and more—she sighed deeply and obeyed the principal's order.

SEVENTEEN

Poaching for Profit

Alti Vincent earned all conference honors as a basketball player at a small teachers college. His academic grades fell far short of his ability on the hardwood, but when he sought a teaching and coaching position he was in high demand, especially in the rural towns around the state. There the citizens cared little about Alti's GPA or his ability (really, inability) to teach history, but they did care that, given his basketball knowledge and ability, he might be able to coach their high school team to a state championship.

After a mini bidding war a middle-sized school won Alti's services. His first year of coaching proved a minor disaster. His boys' squad won five games and lost fourteen. He stayed at the school a second year. This time his team won only two games.

Now he was damaged goods, his boys' teams having won seven times while losing thirty times. His contract was not renewed. He found another coaching job at a smaller school but only to coach the girls' team, a considerable comedown in his opinion.

Still, he was coaching. He treated the girls no differently than he had treated his boys' teams, demanding they learn his style of play, barking at them when they took a poor shot or made a bad pass. He found he liked coaching girls. They played hard. They never gave up. They shot free throws better than boys. They could drill three-pointers from far out on the floor. In his first year coaching girls his team finished winning fourteen games and losing but six.

Not a bad record, but not good enough for Alti. He thought about their losses. Why had his girls lost any games?

He hit upon the reason for the losses. Their talent was simply not good enough. He needed girls who could shoot better, rebound better, defend better.

Chapter 17

And then Alti Vincent had an epiphany. He developed a plan to make himself the most successful girls' basketball coach ever in the state. Alti knew that summer basketball programs for girls had gained popularity. Girls' teams were traveling all over the country playing in tournaments.

So Alti went to businesses in his state's two largest cities to hawk his plan, a plan to help the businesses become more visible and more appreciated by their targeted consumers. He asked them to sponsor girls' teams in summer programs. He would coach the teams, and, he promised, he would put together all-star teams that would clobber teams from other states.

That made sense to the businesses. Several signed up to sponsor teams and to pay Alti a decent sum to coach the girls.

Alti did exactly what he had promised. He conducted tryouts and chose the best players for his teams, three teams actually based on age: a novice team ages 11–13, a mid-stars team ages 14–15, and a senior team 16–18. All won in their first summer program year, the mid-stars compiling a record of twenty-seven wins and only two losses. The sponsoring businesses were most satisfied.

Somewhere along in the summer, Alti experienced a second epiphany. As it happened, one of the just-below-the-top-class high schools needed a new girls' basketball coach. Alti went to the school's principal with his promise that were he hired, he would guarantee that his team would reach the state tournament every year.

He was hired. He set out to recruit the talent he needed to fulfill his promise. The school already had the best player in the state, but she needed teammates to pass her the ball, to rebound, to defend.

So Alti sat down with the parents of the other top players in the state. He met with them and with their daughters and laid out the benefits that would accrue to the girls if they enrolled in his high school and were part of the superstar team.

Certain rules set by the state's high school athletic governing body had to be followed. The parents must live in the district; their domicile must be established by a certain date. To stay within the technicalities of the rules, Alti asked the parents, or at least one parent, to move into the district. He assured them they would have work if they moved. He had arranged with the local businesses to provide them jobs.

Three of the state's most talented players did leave their previous high school and enrolled at Alti's school. With four of the state's best players on their team they won all of their games, and thumped their opponent in the state championship game by seventeen points.

The morning after the state win, Alti went to one of the largest high schools in the state, one with only a so-so record in girls' basketball, to suggest to the principal that he, Alti, be hired to coach the girls' team, and that the present coach could be moved to another job.

He made the same promise he had made before. His teams would win.

THE DILEMMA

The principal of the high school, one Dr. Burley Ruskin, knew of Alti's reputation of luring basketball playing girls away from their home districts to play together. He found that practice rather distasteful.

Still, Dr. Ruskin believed that the lured players might benefit from their transfer to a larger school.

However, how would the present girls' basketball coach take her demotion? She might raise some sort of unpleasant ruckus. Too, how would the girls who were displaced from starting positions on the team react?

Yet, he did want a winning team at his school. By association his reputation would be burnished.

Dr. Ruskin thought about the matter: should he recommend to the school board that Alti Vincent be hired?

THE DEBATE

Pro

Yes, by all means he should recommend the hiring of Coach Vincent. What is not to like about the young coach? Indeed, he should be lauded for having developed a system whereby (1) outstanding student-athletes can find success commensurate with their abilities, (2) said student-athletes can receive athletic scholarships to enable them to attend college, and (3) Alti can be noticed by colleges that may offer him a coaching position. Win-win-win.

The most important question to be asked by the principal: how many Vincent recruits will receive scholarships if they stay in their small school? They may play well in the small school—indeed, very well—but they will not be noticed by big-time college recruiters. Alti Vincent's "luring" them to a big school may be worth tens of thousands of dollars to these girls and their parents.

Finally, Alti has put himself in the spotlight, it is true, but what is wrong with that? He has done what any successful young man or woman must do to rise above the herd. He has worked hard. He had come up with a creative solution to help himself and others.

Alti should be admired . . . and congratulated.

And Dr. Burley Ruskin should recommend that Alti Vincent be hired to coach girls' basketball.

Con

My heavens, what Alti Vincent is doing is nothing new. It is as old as organized sports. "Ringers" were brought in routinely by baseball teams to beef up their lineups at the turn of the twentieth century. Those mercenaries received stipends from businesses in the communities for which they played. This is the "new" poaching avenue Vincent is running?

This is an odious little business Vincent pursues. For one thing, it harms the small school from which the talented girl transfers. With her the school might have been competitive in its class. Without her the school may not win even half its games. To whose detriment? To the detriment of the other players in her former school, to the fans in the community, and to the coach who may lose his or her job as a result of Vincent's poaching.

Further, future damage may be in store for Alti Vincent. Because he will have success in state tournaments, a college may hire him to coach, convinced he had superior coaching skills, when, in fact, all he really has is an ability to persuade parents to bask in their children's glory for a year or two.

Finally, harm is done to the players Alti has poached. They will accept college scholarships but most will seldom live up to expectations when they are matched against girls who are taller, faster, and more aggressive. Like everything else, the ability to play basketball is only relative. Most of Alti's stars will last only a year or two in the college that recruited them. Then they will come home, their tails between their legs, their confidence shattered.

No, Dr. Ruskin, you should not hire Alti Vincent. And, oh, by the way, have you looked at all at his ability (really inability) to teach history?

THE RESOLUTION

On the recommendation of Dr. Burley Ruskin, the Board of Education approved the hiring of Coach Alti Vincent by a unanimous voice vote.

EIGHTEEN
Religion, Racism, and Rumor

Morris Goff began his teaching career at Trippler High School in 1975. While the students liked Mr. Goff, no one in the community came to know him very well. He stayed to himself, attending only school functions to which he was assigned, engaging in conversations with parents only on parent-teacher nights. He never attended any of the town's five churches.

On weekends he left town to go to Kansas City. He had grown up there, and he loved the Kansas City professional sports teams, the Royals and the Chiefs. All fine, no problem

Twelve years passed. Morris Goff remained a bachelor, although rumor was in Trippler that he had a girlfriend in Kansas City or perhaps Topeka. Some students claimed he had begun to talk more about Topeka in class.

A few students joked that Mr. Goff might have joined the "freak" church in Topeka.

The Church of the Reconciliation of Diversity, founded by the Reverend Rodney J. Amos, an African American minister, pushed two main planks in the effort to help parishioners get to heaven. Reverend Amos preached that peace and love can be found only when race and ethnicity were blurred to the extent that they were unrecognizable and hence mattered not at all.

He therefore urged his unmarried African American members to marry white or Asian mates. Conversely he suggested his white or Asian members (he counted a few among his flock) to marry African American women.

The second major plank in Reverend Amos's theology taught that Christians had prayed the *wrong way* for centuries, with their heads lowered. Reverend Amos claimed that with the head down the supplicants' entreaties were more readily heard by Satan than by God. That explained why so many prayers went unanswered. The proper way to pray, according to Reverend Amos, was to pray with the face upward, rather than with the face downward.

Further, so the Reverend Amos claimed, the ideal way of praying was to worship six times every twenty-four hours, three times in daylight, three times in darkness, by lying on one's back with hands clasped behind the head.

So, back to Morris Goff. On a Monday following Mr. Goff's telling the students on Friday that he was going to Topeka, a Kansas City newspaper ran a story about the Church of ROD (the Church of Reconciliation of Diversity) (also Reverend Amos's first name).

Along with the newspaper's story was a photo of a white man entering the church. The distinct features of the man stood out clearly—Mr. Morris Goff.

So, my heavens! asked the good citizens of Trippler, did the school's history teacher belong to the Church of ROD? He certainly never attended any of the five mainstream churches in their community.

Then, two weeks later after the matter quieted a bit, two students entered the history classroom without knocking during Mr. Goff's preparation period. There their teacher was lying on his back on a rainbow colored cloth staring straight up praying to Jesus in a loud, clear voice. The two students closed the door softly without disturbing Mr. Goff.

By five o'clock that afternoon fully two-thirds of the community knew that Morris Goff who taught high school history belonged to the Church of ROD.

And more news soon came. In late November the nuptials page of a Sunday Topeka paper announced the marriage of JoJill Washington and Morris Goff. Again a photo went with the announcement. A white man had married a black woman.

That very Sunday evening the bride was seen helping the groom unload their car at his small home.

On Monday the conversation in the town's lone coffee shop focused only on one topic, the marriage of Ms. Washington to Morris Goff. While some of the older men fumed that a black woman would now be living in their community, most of the younger men simply laughed and made jokes about the marriage. Most of them agreed, at least publicly, that Morris Goff could marry whomever he wished. A couple of the women in the coffee shop said they would invite Ms. Goff to their homes.

While many in the small town shook their heads sadly, the history teacher's embracing a "nut" religion and marrying a dark-skinned woman, Mr. Goff might have survived the storm had it not been for the December incident.

Because Mr. Halperin, the physical education teacher, suffered a stomach virus and missed a week of school, other teachers were dragooned into covering his classes. On Wednesday, as Mr. Goff monitored an intramural basketball game, he realized his afternoon daylight prayer time had almost passed. Engaged in their sport, the students would not miss his presence for five minutes. So reasoned Mr. Goff.

He sneaked out of the gym and hustled down to his classroom, now empty, to grab his Rainbow Cloth and recite his prayer.

All fine, except that as soon as Mr. Goff left the gym a student attempting a layup slipped and rammed his head against the metal support behind the goal. He collapsed and lost consciousness. The students panicked as they looked for Mr. Goff to give them direction, and he was nowhere to be seen.

Everyone in the Trippler community soon knew that Mr. Goff had left his post to pray his "crazy prayer."

A special meeting of the Trippler Board of Education was called.

THE DILEMMA

The Trippler Board of Education met until one o'clock in the morning. Thirty-five patrons demanded that Mr. Morris Goff be terminated immediately. Ten citizens—eight women and two men—all of whom had been Mr. Goff's students, advocated for his retention.

The board members not so much argued, as considered the matter.

Mr. Goff had tenure. He had been a good teacher, not great perhaps, but good enough.

He practiced a "weird" religion. He had left his post.

And at nearly one a.m. the president of the board asked: should we terminate Mr. Morris Goff?

THE DEBATE

Pro

Yes, Mr. Goff must be terminated even though he has taught twelve years in Trippler and the students like him. He has become radicalized and embraced a truly "weird" and unacceptable religion.

While freedom of religion is guaranteed by the Constitution, it does not mean that religious practices that interfere with the basic day-to-day activities of the school are inviolate. Were a Muslim teacher to demand the right to pray five times a day, some of those times during her assigned classroom times, accommodation could be made but would not be required by law to be made.

Moreover, a potential danger exists if Mr. Goff is permitted to practice his rituals unrestricted. It is possible that some of his students, minors, will be attracted to his offbeat religion. While every man or woman has the right to choose his or her own religious belief, it is important to note the emphasis is on "man or woman," not on "boy or girl." High school students are realistically too young to settle upon a belief that is important to their lives.

This case may attract litigation; however, in the best interests of the students of Trippler High School it is imperative that Mr. Goff be terminated.

Con

Now, let's see, what has Morris Goff done over a span of twelve years to merit his termination? He left his duty station for five minutes as he watched over the students of another teacher. What else? Nothing else. Not one thing else. Now that is a pretty good record, a record enhanced by the fact that he is well-liked and respected by almost all of his former and current students.

There are really two *true* reasons why the thirty-five patrons who appeared at the school board meeting to demand his dismissal want Morris Goff gone. The first is his new-found religion. We have seen discrimination against various religions from the Quakers to the Mormons to the Scientologists. Those who are *absolutely certain* they hold the "revealed truth" will always find fault with any different religion, irrespective of the fact that it does no conceivable damage to them. How do the Reverend Rodney Amos's teachings harm anyone, especially since they are much in the same vein as the teachings of Christ?

The second and perhaps the most compelling reason for the thirty-five to want Morris Goff gone is that he married a *black woman!* He is *guilty of miscegenation*.

Although America has come a considerable distance toward racial equality, a significant number of people cannot abide the thought of a black and a white marrying for love. Had Morris Goff adopted Reverend Amos's beliefs without marrying a black woman, the likelihood is that few of Trippler's citizens would have objected to his continued teaching in their school.

Morris Goff is an asset to the Trippler community. There is no possible legitimate cause to dismiss him.

THE RESOLUTION

After the long night of discussion the Board of Education of the Trippler School District voted to retain Mr. Morris Goff.

(Many later believed they voted as they had because they feared litigation from African American groups or various freedom-to-worship groups more than they feared litigation from the still not mollified citizens of their community.)

NINETEEN
The Power of Money

Janet C. grew up rich. Her great-grandfather had established a very successful international shipping business around the turn of the twentieth century.

A brilliant student, Janet could have chosen from dozens of job opportunities following her graduation from college; however, she chose to teach in an inner city middle school. Because her Greek last name was difficult for her students to pronounce, Janet asked to be called Miss C. She taught three classes in earth science and two in place geography.

Before and during college Janet had traveled to many parts of the world. Perhaps because of her experiences abroad she believed knowledge of place geography useful and fun.

The school district ran an annual geography bee, similar to a spelling bee, in which students from the nine middle schools in the district would compete for a small trophy and the title of Geographic Locations Champion (GLC).

By nature competitive, Janet determined that her team of three students would win the GLC trophy. However, soon after her classes began she realized that few of her students shared her curiosity about other countries, cities, oceans, and the like.

She tried every trick she knew to pique their interest, telling them stories about the exotic places she had been, the outdoor markets in Morocco, the yurts in Kyrgyzstan, the bullet trains in Japan. While the students liked her stories nothing seemed to stick with them. When she asked the location of the Baltic Sea they might misplace it near Gibraltar, or if asked about the Solomon Islands they might put them down in the Caribbean.

Then in October before the geography bee in December, she had an inspiration. Her students from the inner city were uniformly poor. Money might motivate them. Money *would* motivate them. She had plenty of money. She would reward her students with money if they could mark the correct locations.

She announced the Pennies for Places program. She would name a country or a U.S. state, and the student must name a bordering country or state—e.g., if she said Germany the student could reply France or, alternatively, Austria or Poland.

She would provide a list of fifty geographic locations. If a student could list all of the abutting locations he or she would win fifty cents. Soon all of her little geography nerds were winning fifty cents a day. By late November she was paying out between eighty and one hundred dollars a week in money earned. That bothered her not at all. She had plenty of money.

Because several of her students were tied with perfect scores after a test she gave, she drew three names out of a hat. Those were her three entries in the geography bee.

In the sixteenth round of the bee one of her students was eliminated when he named Manchester rather than Concord as the capital of New Hampshire. Her other two entries stayed through the thirty-second round before one gave an incorrect answer. Her third entry, a shy little girl named Roxanna, won on the thirty-sixth round when she knew Lake Superior to be the second largest natural lake in the world.

The day after the geography bee Janet C. hosted a glorious pre-Christmas party in the lunchroom after school. Janet paid for all of it.

Although other teachers were invited to the party, only a few came.

Several who did not attend said she had "bought" her students' victory.

The next day Mr. Matlin, the principal, called her to his office.

THE DILEMMA

Mr. Matlin congratulated Janet on her students' performance. They obviously knew a great deal about geographical facts and locations, but he explained that a number of teachers were somewhat upset that she paid students for their knowledge. They could not afford to pay their students, and that seemed unfair to their students and to them.

He wondered what to do: should he ask her not to pay her students anymore? Perhaps he should.

THE DEBATE

Pro

Of course he should order her to stop paying students for knowledge.

What Janet has done in her obsession to taste glory through her students' efforts is exactly akin to a cyclist or a baseball player gaining an advantage through the use of performance enhancing drugs. Her students, coming from homes bereft of money, swiftly became "addicted" to dollars, therefore of course they performed at a higher level than they otherwise might have. Had the competitors from other schools been given money for correct answers, too, in all likelihood Janet's student would not have won the geography bee, it being stated at the outset that her classes performed poorly when provided other non-monetary incentives.

As a culture are we now so far removed from the idea of "learning for learning's sake" that we must now resort to bribery? That is what Janet has done, bribed her children to learn. Soon we will be paying college athletes to play. Of course, in a variety of ways, scholarships, meal money, tutors, they are already paid. But there are plenty of advocates around presently who say give the star quarterback or the play maker point guard cold, hard cash right out in the open. Is our culture rapidly embracing Gordon Gekko's declaration that greed is good?

And one more important question: what if the teachers in other schools whose students competed in the geography bee were not as independently wealthy as Janet? What if they could not afford to pass out hundreds of dollars a week to their students for correct answers? They would be at a big disadvantage, wouldn't they?

Another point: would not a "money for right answers" culture encourage cheating? An example: Ken and Ruth are studying together. The question arises: what is the capital of Nebraska? Wanting to distance himself slightly from a competitor Ken tells Ruth it is Omaha when he knows it is really Lincoln.

What adjectives should be used to describe what Janet has done? Unethical, unjust, immoral, unconscionable, irresponsible . . . oh, the list could go on and on.

Con

Janet should be congratulated for hitting upon the *best* and *most effective* means of improving American education, particularly in our poorest performing schools. Gordon Gekko said, "Greed, for lack of a better word, is good. Greed is right. Greed is good. Greed is right. Greed works." Well, that seems so brutal, doesn't it? But it is so. At least it is so in a capitalist economy. If you term the desire to make money "greed," then almost everyone in America is greedy. Why shouldn't school students be permitted—and even encouraged—to participate in capitalism—in greed.

Were all American students paid to learn, our students would learn more rapidly and more thoroughly than they are learning now. By far.

And, as noted in the previous paragraph, *particularly in our poorest performing schools*. Janet's students provide a glowing example of this.

Of course not all teachers, in fact very few, are in a financial position to pay their students to learn. Either state or federal government money should be provided to every school in America to pay students right from kindergarten through the twelfth grade. Ohhh! The cries can already be heard. How on earth could we get the money necessary to implement this outrageous practice?

Well, I'll tell you how. It is quite simple. Taxes. We will fund the program through taxation. And from where will the taxes be derived? Oh, from the lesser funding needed for prisons—because better educated students are less likely to commit crimes. Oh, from additional tax monies gleaned from the higher paying jobs held by better educated students. Oh, from the reduced funding needed for welfare programs.

Certain matters would need to be considered and determined, matters such as how much students should be paid to make the program fair and equitable. Should kindergarten children receive pennies for learning while high school students receive dollars, that sort of thing? But that can be done. The important point is that we decide to implement the pay for learning program, and then *do it!*

Thank you, Janet, and again, congratulations to you and your students.

THE RESOLUTION

Mr. Matlin asked Janet not to pay her students. She attempted to explain the reason why to her students. They were not happy at all. And their academic work suffered.

TWENTY
Buffaloes and Free Throws

Gary Ray Gompert rose rapidly in the ranks of education and became a high school principal at age thirty-four.

Gary Ray's educational philosophy was simple enough. Create wonder in kids which in turns creates curiosity which then promotes learning, W=C=L.

Thus when Gary Ray became a high school principal he sought to instill his philosophy in his teachers. Not all bought it. Several who had been at the school more than a decade had seen quite enough of the educational philosophy stuff, the fads and fancies, the nostrums served up by the researchers at teachers' colleges who then went into the hinterlands in an uppity manner to tell the old hand teachers how they had been failing to properly instruct their students for lo these many years, and here was how successful teachers did things. All BS, the older teachers believed, the ones who had been on the firing line for years.

Gary Ray sought to install his W=C=L philosophy by recommending to his school board that "outside experts" come into the school to instill wonder in the students. To this end he persuaded the board to approve two national assembly companies bringing programs to the school, the rationale being that the students would be inspired by the wonder demonstrated by the assembly presenters.

The school board bought his argument.

The first assembly featured a trained buffalo named Flossie. Well, Flossie did produce a certain wonder coupled with high hilarity when she relieved herself on the gym floor in the middle of the presentation.

In the second assembly a grizzled old man of seventy-three years clad in a pair of old style brief briefs, floppy socks, and high top shoes tottered out onto the gym floor to demonstrate the proper way to shoot free throws. This assembly did interest the students and evoked some wonder in them. How could this white-haired old fossil possibly make twenty-five free throws out of twenty-five attempts? But he did.

The third assembly featured a husband and wife team, both "little people" less than five feet tall. While the wife played rag time tunes on the piano, her husband danced enthusiastically on top of the piano. At one point the husband slipped and fell off the piano. He gamely rose and leaped to the top of the instrument again and continued to dance. The students gasped when he fell and then laughed uproariously at his recovery.

All in all, the assemblies *did* present real talent and most *did* evoke a greater or lesser wonder in the students; however, as the programs continued, the older teachers became more and more disgusted, resentful that their classes were disrupted so often by "junk."

A teachers' committee went to Gary Ray to ask that he cancel the remaining assemblies. He refused. They returned, this time *demanding* he cancel them. He refused again.

The old-timers then met with the school board threatening "some sort of action" unless the assemblies were halted.

THE DILEMMA

Should future assemblies be canceled?

THE DEBATE

Pro

Yes, the older teachers are right. The upcoming assemblies should be canceled. The types of programs described provide little real educational value for students. Of course the teenagers laughed when the "little person" fell from the piano, but what did they learn from that . . . except possibly not to attempt to dance on top of a piano?

Likewise the buffalo assembly provided amusement, but at the expense of losing an hour during which time science students might have studied the way chemicals interact, and math students might have been studying trigonometry.

As for the free throw expert, all well and good, except it is a dead sure cinch that none of the high school players will ever copy the old man's method of shooting free throws underhanded, a style not used for ninety years.

There is entirely too much emphasis on the "let's soft soap, easy ride, giggle, giggle, learning is big fun" education style these days instead of the "put your nose to the grindstone and really learn something" method used in the past. The latter way *did* work.

Con

Question: how do we learn? Answer: basically there are only two reasons why and how we learn anything. We *can* learn through coercion, the old teachers' method, that is true; e.g., "You are going to learn this formula, by jeez, or you'll get an F, so there, you whelp!"

Or we can learn through curiosity; e.g., "What will happen if I change my grip on the golf club? Hmm."

Which method leads to *real* learning? Well, both can work, but learning by being genuinely curious works far better. Think about it. How many algebraic formulas do you remember? You may remember many, a whole lot, *but only if you were genuinely curious about mathematics*. Most high school graduates, all of whom were required to take algebra, remember very little of it five years after graduation. Why? Because they did not see it as having any relevance to their lives.

So how do you make kids really curious? Kids respond to the new and unusual. So there was a trained buffalo in the gym. Yes, the students laughed, but surely some were really curious about how you train a buffalo . . . or by analogy a horse or a dog or a baseball player (Wonder=Curiosity=Learning).

My gosh! How many free throws in a row can that old geezer make? Maybe he *does* have a better way of shooting than I do. I'll do some research. And . . . I find that one of the greatest free throwers of all time in the National Basketball Association was Rick Barry who shot free throws exactly the way the old geezer did.

Gary Ray has the right method to use to teach children. The difficulty he finds—and many more principals around the country find—is a lack of cooperation from far too many teachers, a reason we desperately need teachers who understand and appreciate how students learn.

Yes, keep the assemblies, school board.

THE RESOLUTION

Although most of the school board members doubted the value of the assemblies, they voted to continue them as scheduled. They felt they could not dare break the contract they had already signed.

TWENTY-ONE
Snake!!!

In college Trudy Jenstrom majored in biology, but when she went out on her first teaching assignment in Rutherford High School, student population ninety-two in grades nine through twelve, she taught all of the science classes offered including biology, ecology, a smattering of both physics and chemistry, and whatever else fell in between.

Students looked forward to Ms. Jenstrom's classes. She knew how to keep their interest. How? She coupled genuine learning with her little "jokes." The students never knew when or how or in what form the "jokes" might surface. For instance, to teach something about electricity Trudy might use a Leyden jar or some other "juice" to surprise an unsuspecting student with a sudden shock when they chanced to touch some innocent appearing object.

Those unaffected by the "jokes" laughed uproariously at the student affected. Most of the time the teen upon whom the joke had been played took little umbrage and accepted his/her victimization in good humor. Trudy always reminded the students that the "joke" illustrated a lesson about to be learned. And such was the case. She built her lessons around her "jokes."

All went well until she taught a unit about zoology. As the class began, Trudy picked up a small box and asked the students if they knew the meaning of the word "herpetology." None did.

She asked them to guess the meaning, giving a hint that it would be the pet (her-pet) a girl might least want. The guesses came: a frog, a skunk, a chameleon. None right.

Trudy stepped close to a senior named Bart McCord aka The Bruiser because of his bantering, battering ways. While The Bruiser secretly annoyed most of his male classmates, they hesitated to cross him lest he pound on them—and not gently either. The girls thought The Bruiser handsome, but his aggressive ways caused them to shy off, too. In their heart of hearts most of his classmates hoped The Bruiser would get his comeuppance someday.

And this day he did.

Trudy placed the small box on The Bruiser's desk and asked, "Do you have a guess, Bart?"

The Bruiser did have a guess. In his superior way he said, "Girls are all scared to death of snakes. I guess you've got a snake in there."

"So you'd say a snake?" asked Trudy.

The Bruiser nodded smugly. "Yeah, that's right. A snake."

"So you say SNAKE!" At the precise moment she shouted the word Trudy opened the box out of which sprang a large, fearsome looking snake aiming its fangs straight at The Bruiser.

"Holy jeez!!!" yelped The Bruiser as he dived onto the floor.

Of course the snake that had scared The Bruiser half to death was one purchased at a practical joke store, but it achieved a result greatly appreciated by The Bruiser's peers. They roared with laughter. And jeered.

Rising to his feet, The Bruiser glared at his still-laughing classmates. Most quieted quickly. One, a nerdish boy named Toby Cloade misjudged The Bruiser's mood a bit. He kept laughing, snorting in a pig-like way as The Bruiser approached. The Bruiser thereupon turned Toby's desk over with Toby still in it. With force.

Toby's head struck the back leg of Peggy Kerwin's chair inflicting a three-inch-long gash in the boy's skull and giving him a concussion.

Although Trudy apologized profusely to Toby and his parents, the parents filed a sizeable lawsuit, not against The Bruiser at all, but against Trudy Jenstrom and the school district. Before a trial occurred, a settlement was reached, the terms not revealed.

THE DILEMMA

Among other questions the school board members had to make a decision about this question: should Trudy Jenstrom be retained for a second year? After considerable discussion they decided to postpone their decision for one week.

THE DEBATE

Pro

Yes, she should be retained. What happened is regrettable, but it was not Ms. Jenstrom's fault. The fault lies entirely with The Bruiser. He and/or his parents should have been the ones paying the cost of Toby's medical bills. Ms. Jenstrom had no way of knowing that The Bruiser would react in the way he did. She had used "interest grabbing techniques" many times before in the classroom without accidents. She had expected The Bruiser to take his ribbing with good humor.

Ms. Jenstrom is clearly a creative and successful teacher, the sort that American education needs in greater numbers.

Con

While a mild practical joke might be tolerated now and then, such shenanigans as that perpetrated by Ms. Jenstrom had no place in the classroom. She should have realized that her "jokes" were certain to cause trouble sooner or later. Teenagers are particularly sensitive to being laughed at or mocked, and many respond poorly, some by silence, others by acting out aggressively as The Bruiser did, and a few even by committing suicide.

One other problem with Ms. Jenstrom's "joke" approach: students will be looking for the "joke," and be less likely to take the subject matter seriously.

There are plenty of other more acceptable ways to interest and educate students without using Ms. Jenstrom's methods.

Trudy Jenstrom should *not* be retained.

THE RESOLUTION

To the relief of the school board members, Trudy Jenstrom resigned within one week of their first meeting to discuss her retention. By the next summer she had received an offer from the National Science Foundation to present science programs in high schools across the country.

TWENTY-TWO
Making the Tackle

After a stint of teaching six years in a large city school, Alvin Stanley followed his wife to a small Nebraska town when she decided to practice family medicine. He found a teaching job at tiny Moncrief High School with only forty-seven students.

The school played eight-man football. Only fifteen boys were on the team. To permit his team to practice eight-on-eight Coach Jules Archer put on a uniform and lined up at running back for the non-starter squad. The first team accepted the necessity of the coach running the ball—they needed the practice—but no one wanted to tackle him. Coach Archer ran hard. Two years before in college he had led his conference in rushing. Short and compact, he made much of his yardage by bowling over would-be tacklers. He continued his running style when he practiced with his high school players.

Moncrief's first string played well, winning their first three games. On the fourth week of the season Moncrief had an open date. Coach Archer felt his boys must have one all-out, game conditions, scrimmage that off week.

The day before the scheduled practice a key defender from the first string came down with the flu. Now, even with Coach Archer playing, there would be only eight against seven.

THE DILEMMA

As the coach lamented this cruel stroke of fate, Alvin Stanley had a capital idea pop into his head. He had played football in high school. He had been out of high school only ten years. He ran every day and lifted weights three times a week. He was well conditioned.

He could suit up and be part of the practice the next day. He could help his friend Coach Archer.

The coach agreed to the idea. He found a uniform, a helmet, and some pads for Alvin.

Alvin promised the coach he would be ready and would play hard.

But when Alvin ran the idea of his suiting up past his wife that evening, she expressed doubt that he should play football with the high school team, even if it was only practice. She pointed out the danger of injury.

Well, of course she would, he thought. She was a medical doctor.

She and Alvin argued. "Yes," he said. "No," she said. Adamantly!

Toward morning, upset by the disagreement with his wife whom he dearly loved and was quite reluctant to disobey, he considered breaking his promise to Coach Archer.

A dozen times he vacillated. Should he play football with the high school team?

Should a teacher do that?

THE DEBATE

Pro

Of course there is a small threat of injury to Alvin.

But the benefits of suiting up to practice with the high school football team are so much greater than bowing to the small threat of injury that there is little comparison.

The idea that teachers should hold themselves far above students is ridiculous. The teacher who talks to his students, who laughs with them, who interacts with them, who is a role model, is going to influence them much more than the teacher who sets himself/herself on a pedestal.

The same is true in every venue of life. The father who plays catch with his son or daughter; the mother who goes swimming with her son or daughter; the business executive who manages by walking around the plant floor and visiting with his/her workers; the doctor who spends an extra five minutes visiting with a patient—all are going to be more respected, admired, and heeded than the one who by action (or inaction) says in effect, "I am superior to you."

Con

Irrespective of his promise to his friend Coach Archer, Alvin should definitely *not* practice with the team. The threat of injury, while present in any full scale blocking and tackling football practice, is a secondary consideration.

The more important consideration is the inevitable erosion of Alvin's dignity. Students must respect teachers, which means they must look up to them. Students must even fear teachers to some degree, and when a teacher puts himself/herself on the same plane as the students the fear evaporates. Teachers are much in the same position as parents in that they should be friendly but not friends.

No, Alvin, you should not have been on the football field with your students.

THE RESOLUTION

The first few minutes of the scrimmage went well for Alvin. He tackled the second-string quarterback for a loss. He batted down a pass. His fake rush caused an opposing player to jump offside.

Then Coach Archer, working with the second team, took a direct snap from center and rolled left. He dodged two defenders and had gained full momentum when he came face to face with Alvin. Coach Archer did not slow or attempt to sidestep Alvin. To have done so would have sent the wrong message to his players, the right message being: football was a tough, hard hitting game, and you slam though anyone in your way, even if he is your math-teacher friend.

Neither did Alvin turn away from attempting the tackle. Football is a tough, hard hitting game, and you tackle the ball carrier, even if he was your head-coach friend.

Coach Archer crashed into Alvin with such force as Alvin had never experienced. Alvin went to the ground. Coach Archer continued down the field.

After a trip to the hospital where another doctor, not his wife, set his broken collarbone, he remained confined to bed for a day. He missed school Monday and Tuesday of the following week.

When he returned to his classes on Wednesday, the students cheered when he entered the classroom. He had achieved hero status.

Later that day the school's principal called Alvin to his office and rebuked him for agreeing to practice with the football team.

TWENTY-THREE
Genius in the Classroom

In her nineteenth year of teaching U.S. history in an Arizona high school Angela Turner experienced the first real stress she had ever felt in the classroom. The stress came from an unexpected source—a genius student.

As that year's fall semester began, Angela liked what she saw: small classes, serious students. Her ten o'clock class included a boy who sported a perfect 4.0 grade point average, certain to graduate the valedictorian of his class. He expressed a desire to attend an Ivy League school, and his chances of that seemed excellent.

In short, Allen Riesman was a genius. All of Angela's colleagues who had had the boy in class said so.

They all disliked Allen Riesman. Intensely.

In the early weeks of the semester Angela could not see why her fellow teachers had been so down on Allen. True, he sneered at his peers when they blew an easy answer. Too, he sighed heavily and exhibited a "can't you come up with something harder?" expression when she asked him a moderately difficult question. He performed brilliantly on tests, coming up with spot-on, detailed answers.

One day in the faculty lounge Angela asked her colleague Millie Santana why teachers disliked Allen.

Millie explained, saying, "Allen is a terribly insecure young man. He must prove he knows more than anyone else, especially in situations when he fancies himself up against someone who is quote, 'an expert,' unquote in his or her field. Like a teacher. He believes proving the expert wrong makes him shine. Actually, of course, it just makes his teachers and the other students in the class think he's a giant butthole."

"He hasn't seemed that way to me," protested Angela.

Millie laughed. "You haven't reached your area of expertise yet, have you? He knows you are an authority on the Civil War. Let me know what happens when you get there."

Indeed, Angela's specialty was Civil War history. She had walked the route of Sherman's March to the Sea. She had done her master's degree thesis on it. She had served as a panel member on a national conference focused on Civil War history.

Two weeks before Christmas the unit on the Civil War began. The third day into the unit Allen Riesman began his assault, his first question being, "Had Albert Sidney Johnston not been killed, would the South have won at Shiloh?"

Angela admitted she did not know. Unfortunately she added her opinion that A. S. Johnston was a successful general. She sensed Allen thought so, too.

She sensed wrong. Allen sprang, saying, "A good general? Do you really think so, Ms. Turner? He divided his forces between Fort Donelson and Nashville in February of sixty-two, thus insuring Grant's victory. I don't think he was a good general at all."

Angela tried to agree with him. "No, I guess not . . . ."

He would not let her get off that easily. "Why not?"

The bell rang ending the period. Angela went to her friend Millie and explained what had happened.

Millie nodded. "That's Allen. He'll keep doing that until you are utterly humbled. He crushes you right in front of the other students."

"So what do I do?" asked Angela.

"Pray for the end of the semester. That's all you can do."

Allen Riesman's attempts to show his superior knowledge, mostly successful efforts, continued beyond the Civil War unit.

THE DILEMMA

Angela Turner was stressed. What could she do? Could she ask the principal to remove Allen from her class, charging . . . what? That he was too smart? Ridiculous!

On the other hand, she doubted her psyche could survive the "Allen assaults."

She wondered: should she tolerate him, *could* she tolerate him, until the end of the school year?

THE DEBATE

Pro

Angela Turner, who believes herself quite knowledgeable about American history and particularly about Civil War history, is stressed because her student asks her questions she cannot answer? Isn't that what students are supposed to do: ask questions? Isn't that what students should be *encouraged* to do?

Clearly Allen Riesman is brilliant. Also, quite clearly, he is different from other students. He may even be considered eccentric, but then aren't most geniuses different or eccentric?

For a moment let us suppose the great genius Nikola Tesla had been in Ms. Turner's class, would she not have thought him "different" (and probably obnoxious)? She would have thought him incredibly different, yet his genius gave us alternating current.

Students like Allen Riesman must be tolerated and encouraged. They are the Teslas, the Edisons, the Zuckerbergs, the Bill Gateses of the world.

Ms. Turner should be thankful that she is so fortunate as to have a genius in her class. Not only will her students learn more than they would have had he not been in the class, but, also possibly, years from now he may even credit her with assisting him along his path toward achievement.

Con

The case of the Genius in the Classroom is all too frequently seen in American schools. Allen Riesman may be brilliant, but his persistent efforts to demonstrate his brilliance cannot be permitted to disrupt the orderly flow of classroom discussions.

He is not helping the other students in the class learn more. He is inhibiting their learning. Whatever arcane knowledge he imparts will not be retained by his peers. Indeed, it will be vehemently rejected because they dislike him.

Surely he has been counseled before about his unacceptable classroom behavior, and the counseling has done little or no good. It is obvious that Allen has a very high IQ, but it is equally obvious that he is plagued by some strain of mental illness that causes him to need to show off his superior intellect and knowledge.

Ms. Turner should speak to the school principal about her growing inability to handle the stress created by the resident Genius in the Classroom. If nothing is done, she must seek other avenues of escape, speaking to the boy's parents, visiting with the district's psychologist (if there is one), absolutely demanding he be transferred to another class.

Angela Turner simply cannot tolerate Allen Riesman's continued presence in her class.

THE RESOLUTION

Angela did speak to the school principal about Allen Riesman. The principal asked Angela to which of her colleagues' classes she proposed they transfer Allen, pointing out that he would inevitably act out in a new teacher's class just as he acted out in hers. She had no answer to that.

The principal explained that he had gone to Allen's parents two years earlier to discuss the young man's classroom behavior. The parents had become quickly angered by any criticism of their son and threatened to sue the teachers, administrators, the school board, and anyone else remotely connected with the school were Allen hobbled in any way in his effort to get into Harvard.

Angela Turner did what her colleague Millie had suggested earlier: she prayed the year would end.

Allen Riesman remained in her class and continued as before.

At last the year did end.

TWENTY-FOUR
The Hunter

Susan Sullivan, a math teacher at Sylvan Woods High School, drew front yard duty on a Monday in mid-October, the duty being little more than watching as the students, most of them, drove into the parking lot and parked. A few exited a school bus, but most drove their own cars.

As Ms. Sullivan stood talking to one of the students, a senior named Ralin Seaman drove up. He got out, stretched, said good morning to Ms. Sullivan and several other students, and opened the trunk of his car to remove his football jersey. The school's quarterback, Ralin had led his team to six straight victories.

But Ms. Sullivan noticed more than just the football jersey. Ralin Seaman had a gun in his trunk.

Sylvan Woods had a *very strict* policy that *no one* would be permitted to have a gun on school property. To possess a gun would automatically mean suspension for at least a week.

Ralin Seaman maintained an A average in Ms. Sullivan's calculus class. Ralin Seaman's parents were close friends of Susan Sullivan and her husband. They frequently partied together. Ralin Seaman was unquestionably the most popular senior boy in the high school.

But there was that *strict policy* about guns on school grounds. Were a gun, any gun, to be observed on the school grounds, the fact must be reported to the principal. Immediately!

Ms. Sullivan stepped over to Ralin. He spoke first, asking her if she had enjoyed the Friday night football game, which Sylvan Woods had won easily. She did not reply. Instead she said, "Ralin, you have a gun in your trunk."

Ralin thought a second. Then he remembered. "Oh, yeah, I guess I do. I was pheasant hunting over the weekend, and I guess I forgot to remove my shotgun. I'll take it out when I get home."

Ms. Sullivan swallowed hard and said, "Ralin, I must report that you have a gun on school property. You know what that means."

Ralin immediately became greatly concerned. He pleaded with Ms. Sullivan to say nothing about the gun. He promised again to remove it as soon as possible.

Ms. Sullivan only nodded. She turned away from Ralin and began to walk up the sidewalk to the building.

She entered the building.

Before she entered the principal's office she hesitated.

THE DILEMMA

Ms. Sullivan's dilemma is quite clear. Should she not report that her best student Ralin Seaman, an outstanding young man in every way, has a shotgun in the trunk of his car, or should she follow school policy and report the presence of the gun to the principal?

THE DEBATE

Pro

Yes, Ms. Sullivan must report the presence of the gun.

Let us say that Ms. Sullivan has been policing the parking lot when a sophomore student named Juan Castillo drives up in his 1998 Chevy. Juan comes from a single parent home. He is a new student this year at Sylvan Woods. Some suspect that he and his mother are undocumented. He is a mediocre student.

Juan opens his trunk and Ms. Sullivan spots a .22 rifle there. What does she do? In all likelihood she does not approach Juan to ask why he has the rifle there. Moreover, Juan's mother is not her friend. She has never even seen the woman. Finally, Juan is of no value to the football team. He barely knows what American football is.

So what does Ms. Sullivan do? She hurries right in to the principal's office and reports that Juan Castillo may be on some dangerous mission and the police better be called immediately.

Justice should be evenhanded. If a policy is a policy, enforce the policy. No exceptions!

Con

Ms. Sullivan should hesitate and *think*. She knows Ralin Seaman very well. She knows Ralin is not going to shoot up the school. She knows his explanation of the gun in his trunk is true. He has been hunting. He loves to hunt. She knows that.

And if she does report him, the principal will feel he must suspend the star quarterback on the week with the game with the toughest rival coming up.

Irrespective of the school's policy on guns, doesn't Ms. Sullivan have the right and, indeed, the obligation, to exercise some judgment? Is she nothing more than a robot?

THE RESOLUTION

Ms. Sullivan did not report the gun in Ralin's trunk.

TWENTY-FIVE
The Paddler

Many parents credited McDonald Middle School's Dean of Boys Waldo Knowlton with instilling the discipline and determination in their children that helped those children become successful business people, religious leaders, and athletes despite the school district's extreme poverty.

How did Dean Knowlton instill those qualities? For thirty-one years at the school, lasting into the mid-2000s he enforced a strict code of behavior for "his boys."

Should a boy misbehave Dean Knowlton paddled him. The routine never differed. The miscreant, usually sent to the dean by a teacher, was quietly "spoken to." Then the type of punishment to be administered was discussed by the dean and the boy, with the dean always having the last word, although now and then he could be swayed to a lesser penalty by a boy's plea.

If paddling was indicated, the boy was paddled. Dean Knowlton paddled with a custom-made, hardwood weapon four inches by one-half inch by three feet. The end held by the dean was rounded, the better to get a firm grip, the better to swat harder. Dean Knowlton did swat hard.

The paddling was conducted in a formalized way. The culprit was led into the school's copier room. A teacher was found to witness the punishment. The student lowered his pants, bent forward, grasped a specially made hand hold on the back of the copier door, and steeled himself.

Dean Knowlton announced the number of swats to be administered, from one to eight depending on the seriousness of the boy's transgression. Then Dean Knowlton laid on, hard enough that the one being paddled often cried out.

The punishment carried out, the boy pulled up his pants, accepted some concluding counsel from the dean, and sufficiently chastised, returned to class.

Through most of Dean Knowlton's tenure at McDonald, no parent ever complained about the punishment meted out. Most supported the dean fully.

Until . . . a new resident who fancied herself a civil-rights advocate moved into town. Her son, a seventh grade boy named Luther, sassed Ms. Longbloom, a math teacher who brooked no sass. Luther soon found himself in Dean Knowlton's office condemned to a four-swat paddling.

The next morning Luther's mother appeared at McDonald Middle School threatening legal action unless Knowlton was dismissed immediately. She claimed that no school official had the right to "whip her boy." She carried on about the awful practice of paddling so vehemently that the principal called the president of the school board, and an emergency meeting of the board was scheduled, a public meeting open to all patrons of the district.

Luther's mother made her case quite effectively, comparing the corporal punishment given her son to canings in English private schools, to the "switchings" often given to African American children in the South, and ultimately, to waterboarding.

She charged that such corporal punishment did no good toward improving the behavior of the person punished—that it, in fact, did great harm psychologically. Moreover, she stated in an absolute tone, corporal punishment was child abuse and thus subject to the laws prohibiting child abuse. She would move on to litigation if need be.

At the same school board meeting more than seventy McDonald alumni appeared, including three former professional athletes who said Dean Knowlton had given them a paddling, a deserved punishment, which they felt had helped them in their careers. Several former McDonald students testified in passionate support of Dean Knowlton and his methods of discipline.

THE DILEMMA

After the public part of the school board meeting, the six board members met in executive session to discuss what they had taken away from the public discussion . . . or, as one board member put it, "real fired-up 'I'm gonna smack you 'long the side of the head' arguments."

On the one hand, an overwhelming number of past and present McDonald patrons strongly approved Dean Knowlton's practice of paddling, some threatening to "raise hell" were it not continued.

On the other hand, the board knew that any lawsuit Luther's mother might institute might prevail—probably would prevail—given recent legal opinions.

They discussed the matter until two in the morning when came a final question (although it had been asked several times in earlier discussions). "Should Dean Waldo Knowlton be disciplined or even dismissed?"

THE DEBATE

Pro

Yes, Dean Knowlton should be disciplined, in fact, quite severely. For many years he has physically abused boys. No good comes from physically abusing anyone.

Oh, there are plenty of advocates of physical punishment, ranging from parents who spank their preschool children to high-ranking government officials who condone and endorse waterboarding as a means of extracting information from enemy prisoners. No evidence exists to show that such punishment works, either to cause children to behave better or to gain information.

One more quite relevant point: unless the school board takes appropriate disciplinary action against Dean Knowlton, the district may find itself spending a significant amount of money to settle a lawsuit.

Con

Mr. Knowlton should be lauded and honored for his work in attaining excellence in McDonald Middle School.

In the past, paddling of misbehaving students was a common practice. Educators and parents alike understood that the adage "spare the rod and spoil the child" really was good advice.

McDonald parents, seeing the success of their children beyond middle school through high school, college, and work were wise enough to know that much of the reason for their children's accomplishments could be traced back to Dean Waldo Knowlton and his refusal to tolerate disciplinary problems.

Further, beyond a stinging backside, what damage was done to those punished? Absolutely none. The contention that they were psychologically damaged is pure hogwash. Indeed, a great deal of good was done.

THE RESOLUTION

The members of the school board breathed a collective sigh of relief when Dean Knowlton, citing his age and time in service, voluntarily resigned.

TWENTY-SIX
The Precious Lost Ball

Marcia Bonesteel taught sixth grade in a K–6 school in Iowa. On a summer vacation to Los Angeles she and her husband attended a Dodgers baseball game, and because her husband had gone to high school with one of the lesser executives in the Dodgers organization, they were able to get a baseball autographed by three Dodgers players.

At World Series time that fall, with the Dodgers playing, Marcia remembered the autographed ball. Knowing her class would like to see it she took it to school.

She showed the autographed baseball to the students before beginning class that morning. Knowing her husband's pride in having that ball, she let none of her students touch it. She held it gingerly between her forefinger and her thumb. Her students oohed and aahed over the ball, particularly three boys who were big Dodgers fans. Several wished they had an autographed ball like that.

Just as Marcia was taking the ball back to its plastic container in her desk drawer, the fire alarm went off. A fire drill.

Marcia knew that the principal timed how long it took everyone to evacuate the building. She hastily placed the ball on the corner of her desk and herded the children into the hall and onto the playground.

When the all-clear sounded and Marcia and her students returned to the classroom one of the boys asked a question about fires. Marcia answered the question and went on with a lesson about food safety.

She forgot about the baseball until after lunch. Then she remembered. She turned back to her desk to pick up the ball and replace it in its container.

It was gone.

Nearly panicking, she looked on the desk, on the floor, behind a curtain on the wall behind her desk. No baseball.

She called her students to attention and asked if anyone knew where the ball had gone. None knew. At least no one admitted knowing.

Marcia could only imagine her husband's anger when he learned that she had lost his treasured baseball. He would explode.

The end of the school day was only twenty minutes away. She *had* to find the ball.

Her first thought was that one of the Dodgers-fan boys had hidden the ball in his backpack.

THE DILEMMA

A dozen thoughts whirled through Marcia's mind. While she recalled that four or five years before she had attended an hour-long program on student searches, she could not remember the specific "dos and don'ts," "mays and may nots."

Did the Fourth Amendment limiting search and seizure *always* apply to students, even to students as young as eleven? Did it *ever* apply to students? Did she need a search warrant?

The term "reasonable suspicion"—what did that mean? Was the matter of student safety a concern? Was she putting her teaching career in jeopardy if she searched her students? Was there a difference between searching a backpack and searching a locker?

She *had* to find that autographed baseball. No two ways about that.

She must decide quickly what to do.

She *had* to search.

THE DEBATE

Pro

Yes, she should search the backpacks. She does have reasonable suspicion that the ball has been taken by one of the students. If she does not search, she will not only lose the baseball, causing her husband, as she is well aware, to be furious, but more importantly, causing whoever stole the baseball to be more likely to steal in the future.

The matter of the right to search is not likely to be an issue. First, the students will know very little about their rights under the Fourth Amendment, and while they may—probably will—go home and tell their parents that teacher searched their backpacks, given the explanation of the lost ball, the parents will excuse Marcia's search.

Of course Marcia should make her reason for searching the children crystal clear. It is quite likely that whoever has taken the ball, seeing that he is about to be searched and the ball found, will confess to his crime and produce the ball with the excuse that he only wanted to take it home to show his dad and that he meant to bring it back the next day.

Yes, Marcia should search her students. In the interest of equal and fair treatment it is important that she search *all* of them, but if she does that, there will be no problem.

One more thing: Marcia better hurry with the search. School will be out twenty minutes after she realizes the ball is missing. She risks much more reaction from the pupils' parents if their kids miss their school bus ride home than she will if the search is conducted.

A note: be advised that the foregoing advice is not that of an attorney.

Con

No, Marcia, be careful. Be *very* careful. The Fourth Amendment does apply to student searches in general, but the particular standards applied by the United States Supreme Court to student searches conducted in schools are important to know and understand.

It is unrealistic to expect every teacher to know and understand the Court's rules and standards, but it is not unrealistic for every teacher to know and understand—and obey—the policies toward student searches set by their individual schools.

If a safety matter were the issue, e.g., a student had come to Marcia to tell her another student had a bomb concealed in his backpack, a search would be justified, but the loss of an autographed baseball, though precious in the eyes of Marcia's husband, is hardly justification for a search. If the baseball is truly gone, in all likelihood a simple letter from Marcia to the Dodgers executive who gave his former high school classmate the original ball, telling what happened, will produce another ball signed by the same three Dodgers.

In Marcia's situation safety is not an issue—unless, of course, domestic violence ensues because of her loss of the baseball.

One last thing: if she asks consent of each individual student to search his or her backpack, then Marcia is probably on firm ground legally, though, of course, some of the parents may still take considerable umbrage at having their child suspected of thievery.

It is probably best that Marcia does *not* search every child's backpack. She definitely does not want to search their lockers.

A note: Understand by all means that the opinions expressed are a layman's opinions and are not those of an attorney.

THE RESOLUTION

At last, knowing she did not understand laws, rules, and regulations regarding student searches sufficiently to recognize dangers lurking therein, Marcia did *not* search any of her students.

After school she returned home, alternating between deciding what lie to tell her husband about the loss of his precious baseball and admitting the horrible truth.

Marcia had fallen into deep depression when her phone rang late that afternoon, and a custodian at the school, a young man named Zandor, called to tell her he had found an autographed baseball amid the contents of a trash can from her room when he had emptied it. He thought she might like it returned.

Would she ever! She offered to buy him lunch the next day if he could drop it by within the next hour.

That he did.

When Marcia's husband came home, he went to the transparent box holding his precious baseball and asked her how the children in her class had liked it.

She told him they had liked it. A lot.

TWENTY-SEVEN
The Banned Wife

Wes Edwards, a child of the sixties, came to Taft-Wilson, a medium-sized high school, to teach math in the early nineties. His students liked him and thought him a good and competent teacher. Although he interacted well with his colleagues at school, unmarried, he went to few out-of-school functions.

After his fourth year at Taft-Wilson he begged off teaching in the summer session, saying he planned to get married.

And soon he did return with his bride. She seemed extraordinarily shy, never appearing in public. No one came to know her well. Wes said little about her except that they had grown up together in Oregon. Soon, however, several terms emerged, ones like "ashram," and "yoga" and "guru," and the locals who pried into such mysterious matters concluded that Wes Edwards and his wife—whom Wes called Clover— came from a Hindu or Buddhist hippie commune.

While a few patrons wondered about the wisdom of having a hippie math teacher in their school, most shrugged and adopted a live-and-let-live attitude. Wes Edwards seemed to know his math and taught it well, and his wife bothered no one. Indeed, very few people ever saw her. Sometimes she was glimpsed running on a trail behind the high school, but if by chance encountered there, she never spoke, only smiled, and kept on running.

Then, to everyone's surprise, at a late October meeting of the Taft-Wilson Board of Education, Clover Edwards appeared among the eighteen persons present. She took a seat in the back of the room. For an hour as the board members discussed various topics and listened while two members of a parents' group reported on fund-raising activities, Clover, a very attractive woman with long, flowing hair, and a small beauty mark on her forehead, sat quietly and said nothing.

However, during a noncontroversial discussion about giving free passes to athletic events to senior citizens, Clover interrupted the board president's remarks with several low moans accompanied by small convulsive moves, overt enough to cause the president to stop speaking and to cause everyone to stare at her, wondering if she was all right. When the discussion about the passes for senior citizens concluded, Clover returned to her previous silence and sat through the rest of the meeting.

In the board's November meeting Clover again appeared. This time she seated herself near the front of the room. Nothing untoward happened until the director of food service for the school started her report. At that point Clover Edwards rose, took a few steps to the side of the room, and stood moving her head up and down and making a catching motion with her hands in front of her breasts as if she were vomiting.

For a few moments the assemblage sat in stunned silence. Clover left the meeting quickly thereafter.

In the December board meeting, Clover again was present. At the beginning of a discussion about the purchase of new football equipment, she produced a football helmet, placed it on her head, smacked herself on her forehead, and collapsed onto the floor of the board room.

She rose and returned to her seat where she sat quietly until the representative of a firm contracted to resurface the football field began to speak. Then she leaped to her feet and silently mouthed the question, "Why?"

The contractor's representative stopped in mid-sentence, squeaked "why" himself, and, having no idea how to respond to the interruption, stood completely flustered for a full thirty seconds before he managed to swallow and continue.

Having had more than enough of Clover Edwards's antics, the school board detailed the high school principal, one Jimmy Lee Cogsby, to speak to Wes Edwards about his wife's behavior.

Cogsby called Wes Edwards into his office and asked what the hell was going on with his wife.

In a gentle, reasoned way Wes explained that Clover was merely expressing her views on certain school policies and practices. Because she had grown up in a "women remain silent" ashram, she seldom spoke, but expressed her opinions with gestures and facial movements. When the food service manager had spoken, Clover had been expressing her concern for students being fed cafeteria food, which included meat and sugar, both poisons, she believed. When discussions relating to football were held, she had been protesting that sports took too much time and money and should not be part of a school's program.

Cogby, a no nonsense man, gave Wes an immediate ultimatum. Either his wife stop her bizarre behavior in board meetings or she would be banned from attending.

Wes then pointed out that other school patrons were permitted to levy their protests about various school policies and practices. Why shouldn't Clover be permitted the same right to protest, even if she did protest in different ways than the mass public?

They could forget about banning Clover from board meetings, warned Wes quietly but still forcefully. She had a Constitutional right to be there. He hinted of legal action were Clover removed from the board room against her will.

THE DILEMMA

In executive session the board members wrestled with the Clover problem. If they did ban her from their public meetings, they might run the risk of a lawsuit. While Wes Edwards seemed a quiet, gentle sort for the most part, Cogsby, the principal, assured the board members that the ex-hippie math teacher could be and sometimes was stubborn and demanding. He might sue.

On the other hand, if they did nothing and Clover Edwards continued her preposterous behavior, board room order would soon morph into utter chaos. Other patrons who attended board meetings were thoroughly disgusted and angry. Some of the regulars in attendance had taken to booing and calling for her removal when she began her "protests."

At last the board president sighed heavily and said Clover must be banned from board meetings. Was he correct in banning her?

THE DEBATE

Pro

Yes, of course she must be banned, no ifs, ands, or buts about that. This situation is no different from a heckler attempting to hamstring a political rally.

If Clover would abide by the rules set by the board relating to participation in suggestions and arguments put before the board, if she would simply voice her opinions and not present them in an absolutely absurd way, that would be quite acceptable, but to make strange gestures and grimace when she disagrees with school policy deserves quick and certain censure.

The threat of legal action is silly. No court would even consider the matter.

No, the next time Clover acts up, kick her out. Ban her from the board room. It should be and is a simple matter.

Con

Not so fast. Freedom of speech really means freedom to communicate. If a deaf person should appear at a board meeting wishing to communicate through signing, would he or she be banned from future attendance? If a handicapped person desiring to comment but able to communicate only through a voice synthesizer be banned?

Remember, too, there may be a religious question in play here. Clover is not of a "usual" religion, but has grown up in a commune practicing a "different" faith, one which apparently frowns on women speaking often. So, query, how is she to communicate her protests if not through some other means than speaking?

Before Clover Edwards is banned from board meetings, it should be remembered that she sits quietly and does not disrupt at all until a subject about which she feels passionate is raised, i.e., the kinds of meals served in the high school cafeteria and the role of sports in the school program. Because these topics are not often the focus of the agenda, her protests are actually quite few and surely can be tolerated by all present.

Finally if you do successfully ban Clover from the board meetings, are you not at the very least likely to lose her husband, a teacher the students like and believe is a very good instructor?

No, the question of whether to ban Clover Edwards from Taft-Wilson Board of Education meetings should be considered long and hard before acting.

THE RESOLUTION

The members of the Taft-Wilson Board of Education turned the matter over to the board's attorney. He uncovered a U.S. Supreme Court decision he felt similar to the Clover Edwards matter, *Grayned v. The City of Rockford*, and he advised that Clover Edwards could be legally banned from board meetings. This was done.

Wes Edwards did not carry out his threat of legal action. He resigned at the end of the semester, and he and Clover went away.

And one other interesting tidbit: during the course of the matter it was learned that Wes Edwards's first name was not Wesley, but rather initials standing for Water, Earth, Sun, W. E. S., the name his commune parents had given him.

TWENTY-EIGHT
The Dog in the Classroom

When Rachel Winescot began her fourth year of teaching third graders, she eagerly looked forward to meeting her pupils.

Her love of children prompted the school's principal to assign a certain young boy to her class.

The boy, Elliot, had come to Rachel's school because of a tragic accident in another state. The accident had taken the lives of both of Elliot's parents. He and his dog had survived. Now the boy lived with his grandparents in Rachel's school district.

But . . . a problem. The death of his parents had severely traumatized Elliot. Unless the dog, a large St. Bernard named Brutus, was in Elliot's presence all the time, Elliot became disconsolate and wept uncontrollably.

Elliot was being seen by a child psychologist, and according to his grandmother his state of mind was improving, but he still needed to have Brutus within sight.

At first Rachel welcomed the boy and his dog to her classroom. As a junior and senior in college she had worked with children who had been removed from their parents for one reason or another. She had learned much from that experience she was sure would help her with Elliot and Brutus.

Rachel's third graders welcomed the new boy. Particularly they welcomed his dog.

But soon for Rachel the year became increasingly stressful. Mostly it was the dog. An untrained animal, in fact, a dog barely out of puppyhood, Brutus careened around the classroom drooling in the way of his breed, barking at squirrels and birds he spotted outside the room, and snoring loudly when he slept. Moreover, he had to be taken for walks twice a day. Leon the custodian drew the lot of walking the dog . . . and Elliot. The boy had to be with his dog.

Of course the students' efforts to learn anything was disrupted. When Brutus barked unexpectedly they laughed. While they were supposed to be learning multiplication they were busy petting Brutus. Rachel did her best to deal with the distractions. She could not.

Halfway through the semester Rachel very reluctantly went to her principal to voice her concerns.

THE DILEMMA

Elliot could not function without the dog's presence, but Brutus daily interfered with the pupils' learning.

Rachel asked the principal if Elliot and Brutus could be removed from her classroom.

THE DEBATE

Pro

Sad though it be, Elliot and Brutus should be removed from Rachel's classroom. The decision should be based on simple arithmetic. It is more logical and sensible to respect the needs of twenty children than the needs of one.

The practice of mainstreaming physically or mentally disturbed or handicapped children has become a reason, often a major reason, for the failure of the American educational system to keep pace with other advanced countries.

Through no fault of their own Elliot and Brutus have become constant and significant distractions to the other students. Elliot's traumatic experience is horrible by any measure, but it should not be permitted to also damage the education, and consequently the lives, of other children.

Con

No, for several reasons Elliot and Brutus should *not* be removed from Rachel's classroom. Or, if they are removed, they should be placed in another "regular" classroom.

Why? First and foremost because Elliot and Brutus provide a lesson to the other children, a more important lesson than any other Rachel could teach—the lesson of compassion and caring. Twenty pupils will always remember their friend and his dog and will be better human beings because they do remember.

Moreover, while the dog may interrupt a lesson from time to time with his barking or other antics, the distraction to the other students is probably overstated. Children are remarkably able to compartmentalize.

No, keep Elliot and Brutus in the classroom. It is a blessing to all involved including Rachel Winescot.

THE RESOLUTION

Rachel's principal made arrangements to have Elliot home schooled . . . and Brutus, too.

TWENTY-NINE
The Boy with ESP

For twenty-two years Hannah Frost taught fifth grade without much stress. She liked her students; they liked her. She taught. They learned. No stress.

That all changed when Gregor Zolotov appeared in her class. Gregor and his mother had moved from New York City to Arizona in the summer before Gregor entered Ms. Frost's class.

Actually Ms. Frost met Gregor's mother before she met Gregor. The mother came to Ms. Frost's classroom on a teacher work day a week before school started .

She explained that both she and Gregor were "gifted." They "saw the future."

Ms. Frost had never met anyone who "saw the future." It was with some effort that she restrained her surprise and let Ms. Zolotov continue.

Ms. Zolotov went on to say she had come to meet Ms. Frost to warn her of a possible problem that might arise with Gregor. It seemed that Gregor sometimes became quite agitated and distressed when he saw a bad future for one of his fellow students.

When this happened, Ms. Zolotov further explained, she must be called immediately to come to the school to pick up Gregor before he warned his friend of what bad thing was soon to occur. It was better that the friend did not know, Ms. Zolotov said, because the bad thing was going to happen—it could not be prevented—and the knowledge that it would happen would only serve to upset the one to whom it would happen. No point in giving advanced warning.

Sure she was dealing with a demented woman, Ms. Frost forestalled herself from inquiring further about "seeing the future." She assured Ms. Zolotov she would call if Gregor exhibited the symptoms that had been described.

Ms. Zolotov left.

Ms. Frost found the school's principal and described Ms. Zolotov's visit. The principal listened with increasing interest, but in the end advised Ms. Frost that in all likelihood nothing very serious would happen. If and when it did they would deal with it then.

On the first day of school Gregor appeared in Ms. Frost's classroom. She had no trouble in identifying him. To start with, the boy's physical appearance took Ms. Frost aback a bit. Appallingly thin and pale, Gregor wore his dark hair down to his waist. When she greeted him, welcoming him to the class, he maintained a sober expression. He looked past her—not establishing eye contact, but beyond her—a concerned sort of look on his face as if he were seeing something behind her that troubled him.

As the first few days of class passed, she began to relax. Perhaps the principal had been right—nothing very serious would happen. Indeed, she rather liked having Gregor in her class. He kept to his studies very well, better than most of her other students. And, for a ten-year-old boy, he seemed intelligent. Well, Ms. Frost thought, not merely intelligent—brilliant.

Then it happened. Late on a Thursday afternoon about thirty minutes before school would be dismissed, Gregor began to seem restless. Instead of sitting at his desk and reading as he always did during study time, he rose and went to the window where he stood and stared. Ms. Frost remembered Ms. Zolotov's command to call her if Gregor became agitated. She did not call. School was nearly out and Gregor did not appear unduly troubled.

Ms. Frost went to the same window as Gregor, stood behind him, and tried to determine what he saw. She saw nothing at all unusual. Two women were walking down the street, one of them leading a dog.

Ms. Frost asked him if he had seen something. Yes, he replied, but offered nothing more. Looking more serious than ever, he returned to his desk.

At ten o'clock that night as Ms. Frost graded some homework, her phone rang. The mother of another boy in Ms. Frost's class had a question: what had happened that day to so upset her son, a boy named Timothy?

Ms. Frost had no idea. She asked to know more.

The mother answered. Timothy had come home from school highly distraught. Weeping even. And when she asked what was wrong he said he knew he would have an accident within two months. His friend Gregor had seen the accident before it happened. Gregor had told him.

The next morning Ms. Frost led Timothy into the hall to reassure him that all would be well, that Gregor had seen nothing, that he was only kidding. Timothy nodded soberly. Ms. Frost could tell he didn't believe her.

Over the noon hour Ms. Frost contrived to get Gregor into her classroom by himself. She remonstrated with him for scaring Timothy so. He bit his lower lip, tipped his head to the side, and said, "You know, Ms. Frost, I really can't help it. I have the gift, you know."

"What gift?" she asked, already knowing his answer.

"Extrasensory perception. ESP. Mother and I both have it. I try to keep what I see to myself, you know, but sometimes I slip. I think maybe the thing I see won't happen if the victim knows it's going to happen, you know, maybe he can prevent it. Of course he can't." Gregor shrugged hopelessly.

Not knowing what to say, Ms. Frost asked Gregor to say nothing to any other potential victims. He said he would try not to.

And then exactly one month after Gregor had warned Timothy of his upcoming accident, Timothy fell on the playground at noon while playing basketball and broke his arm.

Two days later when he returned to school Timothy immediately told everyone in the class about Gregor's warning. "He sees the future. He told me he does. He knew I'd break my arm. He told me."

Timothy's "outing" of Gregor caused a high sense of angst among Ms. Frost's students. Despite her best efforts to calm them, every day they kept at Gregor to tell them their fate. His "gift of a third eye," as he described his ability to other students made him unique. And, Ms. Frost could tell, pleased him immensely. He was now the "star."

THE DILEMMA

Ms. Frost believed, of course, that Timothy's accident following Gregor's prediction had been purely coincidental; however, she now had to deal with the concern and fright the other children would feel if Gregor predicted accidents for them.

Actually, aside from the "seeing into the future" stuff, Ms. Frost liked Gregor. He was, she believed, the most intelligent—the best—student she had ever taught, *ever*, in her twenty-two years in the classroom. She really wanted to continue with him as her student.

She debated what to do. Should she ask that Gregor be removed from her class?

THE DEBATE

Pro

Gregor should be removed from Ms. Frost's class, no question about it. He has upset the other students so much that they are beyond help. Because Timothy did suffer the broken arm, the other children now are convinced that Gregor does possess magical powers, that he does know what is to happen to them.

Moreover, Gregor revels in his "stardom." The other children believe him a virtual god, at least a small god, who knows what is coming, and so they at once idolize him and fear him, much in the way that all gods are idolized and feared.

Asking Gregor not to predict will not work. The children will continue to badger him into predictions. While many people say they don't want to know the future, children *do* want to know what is going to happen to them.

Ms. Frost must speak to her principal, and the child must be removed from her classroom.

Con

The situation described is played out in nearly every elementary school across America every day. A student like Gregor will find his or her way to be king or queen of the hill by bullying the other students into believing he or she has some "power."

The other students will run around in a sweat for a day or two or even longer, but they will at last discover that the "king or queen of the hill," the "little god," has flummoxed them for a time, and then they will laugh at him or her.

This scene is one of the most common that exists among grade school children. The only reason it is different in Gregor's case is because Timothy did happen to break his arm within the time frame Gregor gave.

Ms. Frost should come down *hard* on Gregor and tell him he will be gone from her class if he *ever* tells another child about an impending accident. Time will pass. The children will soon get over their fears. All will be well. As stated earlier, this sort of thing happens every day in America's grade schools.

THE RESOLUTION

On a day Gregor was absent because of illness, Ms. Frost told her other pupils that Gregor had no power to see the future, none at all.

Within a month Ms. Frost could see that many of her pupils still believed that Gregor possessed "the third eye."

Reluctantly she asked the principal to have Gregor placed in another class.

THIRTY
A Trip to the Dentist

May Lou Dennison skipped lunch to drive to the home of LeeAvon her third grade student, who was absent from her class but who, the day before, had complained of a bad toothache.

May Lou rang the doorbell of the small house. The door opened. LeeAvon appeared, crying hard. May Lou soon learned that (1) the toothache was worse, and (2) the boy's mother was not home. Nor was anyone else. The little boy was alone.

With some difficulty May Lou learned where LeeAvon's mother worked. She found the phone number and called. LeeAvon's mother had not appeared at work. No one there knew her whereabouts.

LeeAvon cried harder. May Lou sought help, going to the houses of five neighbors. No one seemed to be home.

LeeAvon needed a dentist. There was no dentist in the small town.

THE DILEMMA

The boy needed relief from the pain he was suffering. May Lou considered what to do. She was thankful about one thing: in lieu of a teacher in-service program there were no afternoon classes. She had time.

She could take the boy to the small police station in the town and explain the situation to Beatrice, the 911 lady. While not a dentist, Beatrice might have a drug to relieve LeeAvon's pain, and he could stay at the station with Beatrice until his mother came home.

But a potential problem occurred to May Lou. If she took LeeAvon to the police station, Chief Hanscombe might feel obliged to refer the situation—the mother being gone, the boy alone, all that—to the county attorney. LeeAvon might be taken from his mother and placed in a foster home.

May Lou thought longer. She could load LeeAvon into her car and drive twelve miles to the larger town where there were two dentists. One might agree to treat LeeAvon.

But would he? May Lou realized she would have no standing as a parent or a guardian. They might not be willing to help LeeAvon.

LeeAvon lay on an old sofa, a pillow pulled tight over his head, sobbing convulsively.

May Lou knew she must act.

The dentist? Should she?

THE DEBATE

Pro

Of course she should take LeeAvon to the dentist. Immediately. Get the little fellow some relief. She can explain the situation to the dentist, and if he has an ounce of compassion in his heart he will treat the boy and cause no problem for her.

Because May Lou is a teacher, in fact, the boy's teacher, she will be acting in *loco parentis* (in place of the parent). She is on solid legal ground.

She definitely should not take LeeAvon to the police. They may very well take the boy out of his home and away from his mother. According to May Lou, this would be devastating for the boy. He loves his mother.

Con

May Lou should take the boy to the police. LeeAvon is not her responsibility, and she puts herself at risk if she attempts to act in *loco parentis*. Were she in the school then it might be acceptable for her to treat LeeAvon as if he were her own child, but she is not at school.

And the further question: where is the boy's mother? Has she not abandoned the child, at least in the letter of the law? Why should she not lose custody of the boy? Even though he says he loves his mother, he may be far safer and better cared for if he is taken out of his home.

While it is obvious that May Lou is a caring person, she is not the one who should make the decision about what happens to the boy. She leaves herself open to all manner of charges if she does any more than simply deliver the child to the police station. Were there a hospital in her town, perhaps she could take the child there, but there is not.

THE RESOLUTION

May Lou took the boy to a dentist in the nearby town. He treated the boy.

May Lou then took LeeAvon to his home, but before she let him out of the car she went to the door to see if the boy's mother had come home. She had, and she was frantic over the whereabouts of her son. She ran to the car, hugged little LeeAvon as she bundled him into the house, thanked May Lou profusely, and offered to pay the dentist's bill.

The mother told May Lou a flimsy story about how she had left LeeAvon with a babysitter when she'd gone to a restaurant with her boyfriend, and then they had been in an accident with his car, and the babysitter must have just gone on home, and . . .

May Lou guessed that the mother had been drunk and had spent the night with her boyfriend. She wondered if she should have taken LeeAvon to the police station.

THIRTY-ONE
Climate Change

For the first twenty-seven years of science teacher Henry Lightfiler's tenure at Gossman High School, the curricula director had been Wilbert Bostwick, Henry's friend and hunting companion. Then Wilbert retired and was replaced by a thirty-something fellow named Johnny Pinkham.

Henry was troubled by Pinkham's gung ho enthusiasm, and even more by the new man's habit of leaning on teachers to change what or how they taught. One change suggested to Henry by Pinkham annoyed—really angered—the old science man very much.

Pinkham asked Henry to include a unit on climate change in his science classes.

Henry did not believe there was climate change. Weather changed from year to year, of course, but climate remained constant, so Henry believed.

Oh, Henry knew that ninety plus percent of the world's scientists claimed the world's climate was changing, but Henry believed political philosophy more than scientific evidence influenced them.

Henry felt he had a responsibility to teach the truth. The notion of climate change was only a theory, not a proven fact. Henry elected to ignore Pinkham's proposal that he teach climate change.

When Johnny Pinkham found out about Henry's noncompliance, he first went to Mr. Donlan, the principal, to ask him to speak to Henry. While Mr. Donlan did not feel as passionate as Pinkham about the need to alert students to the world's greatest danger (in Pinkham's opinion), he agreed to speak to Henry.

Chapter 31

THE DILEMMA

Everyone from school board members to the custodians agreed that Henry Lightfiler had been and was an excellent teacher. Mr. Donlan knew that, but the new curricula director Mr. Pinkham remained adamant that climate change *must* be taught.

The dilemma for Mr. Donlan—and perhaps at some point the Board of Education: could Henry Lightfiler be forced to teach climate change? Henry had hinted he might leave teaching and go off to hunt bear in Alaska if ordered to teach a theory he considered scientific nonsense.

Mr. Donlan pondered long. Should he tell Henry he must teach climate change?

THE DEBATE

Pro

Climate change is not merely a theory as Henry argues. It is a proven fact. How many polar bears must die before the world recognizes that the problem is serious—indeed, as Pinkham believes, the most serious faced by mankind.

When we have all of the evidence of the possible extinction of whole species of living creatures, of extreme drought in parts of the world (including California), of oceans warming, and on and on unfortunately Pinkham is right. Climate change *is* the most dangerous threat mankind has ever faced.

We must deal with the threat before it is too late, and therefore our students should be abundantly aware of it.

Henry Lightfiler is right; there are scientists who don't believe climate change is real—about three percent. But so it always is with any scientifically proved fact. Some scientists(?) do not believe in evolution. Some do not accept the fact that tobacco is a carcinogen.

Let us suppose Henry did not believe in gravity. Should he not be required to say anything about gravity in a basic science class? Let us suppose he does believe in aliens visiting earth. Should he teach that to his students?

No, Henry should be asked to teach scientific truths, and if he refuses, well then, perhaps Henry should go off to Alaska to hunt bear. (But he'd better get there soon or they will be extinct.)

Con

Whether Henry is going to teach about climate change or not is really a moot point.

Of course he is wrong about climate change. We are experiencing climate change, no question about that; however, teaching about it or not teaching about it will make no difference at all to the students in his class. They will be able to do nothing about it.

The world has waited too long to address the issue. Possibly we never could have made a difference anyway. The use of fossil fuels was and is simply too simple and efficient to cause industrial nations to forsake them. Even if the United States turned to wind, solar, and nuclear energy sources within the next ten years, say, it would make little difference in the emissions of greenhouse gases. China, India, Russia, and other nations will continue to spew these gases.

Thus, my point is that Henry Lightfiler could devote an entire year to discussing climate change with his students, and nothing would change. The students may learn that mankind is doomed and that they can do nothing at all about it, but of what use is that? They will be made afraid, not for themselves but for their grandchildren or great grandchildren, and conceivably they might elect not to have children or whatever, but nothing can be done to change the fact of climate change.

That being the truth, then why bother Henry by insisting that he include a unit on climate change in his curriculum? It matters not at all whether he teaches about it or doesn't.

THE RESOLUTION

Henry did not teach a unit on climate change in his classes. He agreed to mention it as a theory . . . briefly.

Henry retired at the end of the year.

THIRTY-TWO

Boy or Girl?

One of her fourth grade students dressed and acted like a boy, the teacher Ms. Hamlin, told the Vail-Hyder Superintendent of Schools Dr. Harshman. The girl, Lucy, wore Levi's, played basketball with the boys, and had her hair cut short.

Dr. Harshman laughed and murmured, "A tomboy."

Ms. Hamlin went on to say that Lucy wanted to be called Luke and she insisted on being permitted to use the boys' restroom.

The latter information got Dr. Harshman's full attention. "You don't let her, do you?"

Ms. Hamlin admitted she had let Lucy use the boys' restroom a few times after having a male teacher shoo any lingering boys out. If refused permission, Lucy threw first-class tantrums.

Ms. Hamlin's most serious concern was the unhealthy classroom ambience Lucy created. The rest of her students treated Lucy as a pariah. The boys shrieked if she came near them; the girls behaved slightly better but none befriended her.

Neither Dr. Harshman nor Ms. Hamlin had any ready answers to the Lucy situation. Both knew about transgender children, but neither had dealt with one who demanded boys' restroom privileges.

During the next week Dr. Harshman visited all of the district's seventeen elementary and middle schools. She learned ten of those schools had identified transgender or possibly transgender pupils in their classrooms. She learned, too, that all of the transgender children were routinely bullied and/or shunned to a greater or lesser degree.

THE DILEMMA

Dr. Harshman considered what should be done—if anything. She decided her teachers needed education on how to best create and maintain welcoming classrooms for transgender children.

She looked on the Web and found the names of several experts on transgender subjects, two located quite near her district. Perhaps she could retain one of them to provide a teacher in-service program.

Still, she realized that some parents and some teachers, too, would be disgusted and angered by any effort to run a seminar dealing with a pupil situation they believed occurred very seldom.

Dr. Harshman thought about it for two days. She sought the advice of other educators. None could help her much.

Should she schedule a workshop on transgender matters?

THE DEBATE

Pro

Of course she should schedule the seminar. Most teachers have no idea how to handle situations like that described, which can—and do—create such classroom difficulties.

Think for a moment about poor Lucy's school life. Because of her involuntary feelings, she is shunned or bullied by all her classmates. She cannot "simply be a girl," even when she is virtually ordered "to be a girl."

Most transgender children do not understand why they are different, but they know that they are, and that knowledge is terribly troubling to them.

The parents of transgender children are often frustrated by what they may see as their child's perversion. They do not understand that transgender children are behaving naturally—for them.

Ideally, Dr. Harshman should schedule *two* meetings with the expert, one for the district's teachers and the other for the parents of transgender children.

In any event, Dr. Harshman should make an attempt to make the lives of all children in the district's schools bearable, if not, in fact, pleasant.

Con

While everyone should have sympathy for transgender children as conflicted as Lucy, raising their problems to the level of being worthy of having experts conduct workshops on the topic is likely to do more harm than good.

To start with, very few transgender children are truly transsexual; i.e., they are not so far over to the opposite side of their birth gender that they want a sex change operation. All humans are transgender to a greater or lesser degree. We all have certain male characteristics. We all have certain female characteristics.

Therefore, the only reason to conduct the proposed workshop is to instruct and sensitize teachers on how to create a more comfortable and understanding classroom situation, a noble reason, true, but probably not actually very realistic. Girls who desperately want to use the boys' restroom (Lucy), or vice versa, are going to change little.

And when the media, particularly the media that decries and scoffs at "politically correct" solutions, hears about some of the "experts" methods of remedying classroom problems—like deemphasizing gender to the point of not calling boys "boys" or girls "girls," but using some idiotic, made-up group term like "orange ocelots," they will jeer and gibe and make conditions worse to the point of being intolerable.

As well, the public, most believing transgender behavior is unnatural and even obscene, are likely to sneer and scoff at the Superintendent's efforts even more than the media.

A transgender behaving as Lucy behaves cannot be permitted to remain in a public school classroom. Possibly the best solution for the matter is arrange that Lucy be privately schooled with a view toward a possible sex change in the future.

THE RESOLUTION

Dr. Harshman did schedule a teacher workshop with a transgender expert, but before it could be held, so much disapproval came from the public and media alike that she was forced to cancel it.

Lucy remained in Ms. Hamlin's class . . . still demanding to use the boys' restroom.

THIRTY-THREE
Baggy Pants

For seventeen years Inez Kolenek taught in a parochial high school in which all students were required to wear uniforms. When her husband's employment took them to another state, Inez took a teaching position in a public high school.

While her new school students did not wear uniforms, they were required to abide by a dress code, a code which, in Ms. Kolenek's opinion, gave students too much choice in what to wear.

Many of the boys wore baggy pants, not quite showing their butts though almost, and the girls wore slacks more than skirts. A small clique of boys wore "goth" clothes—all black.

While most of her students in their classroom behavior or their work ethic seemed to be little different from her parochial school students, nevertheless the lack of uniformity in dress caused Inez Kolenek discomfort, believing as she did that certain modes of clothing represented disorder and even possible danger. She believed this enough that she decided to decree her own dress code for students in her classroom.

She announced her code. Students who did not comply would be disciplined.

THE DILEMMA

Mr. Jarvis Peters, the high school principal, expressed his frustration with a huge sigh as he considered the matter.

Mrs. Kolenek's students, most of them, had protested the clothing edict vehemently. Worse, more than half of the students' parents had called Mr. Peters to decry the teacher's clothing rules.

On the other hand, a significant number of parents had called to applaud Ms. Kolenek's decree.

To make matters worse for Mr. Peters, when he had discussed the matter with Ms. Kolenek, she had brooked no compromise, warning that she would resign immediately if he did not support her.

If he nixed Ms. Kolenek's rules, she would quit. If he did support her rules, her students and some of their parents would revolt.

Mr. Peters considered: should he negate Ms. Kolenek's dress code or . . .

THE DEBATE

Pro

Mr. Peters should never permit the dress code for one classroom to be different from that of another. The school has a dress code that should be observed. The puritanical moral code of one teacher should not supersede the school's dress code policy. Whether the school's dress code is too liberal may be debated, but as long as it represents the school board's policy, it is the policy for the entire school.

Another question—the really important question—is: can it be demonstrated that the dress code present in this high school leads in any way to greater immorality or criminality on the part of students than the uniform dress code found in parochial or private schools?

If observed, Ms. Kolenek's students will be subject to teasing and perhaps bullying by their unhampered schoolmates. This is not an insignificant point.

Most of Ms. Kolenek's students resent the rule, and she will "lose" them. They and she will become foes more or less, a definitely unhealthy atmosphere in which to learn.

Restricting reasonable clothing preferences angers teenagers. Many will argue that conservative dress codes stifle their individuality.

Mr. Peters should absolutely forbid Ms. Kolenek from designing and insisting on her own dress code.

Con

While I do not suppose that Ms. Kolenek can prevail in her quest to bring suitable dress to her classroom, she is to be lauded for making the effort. There are many public school teachers, perhaps most, who wish that all students would be expected to wear uniforms.

If uniforms were made mandatory in all schools, many problems and potential problems would be avoided. In the Columbine, Colorado, shooting a few years back there has been speculation based on sound evidence that the two killers were bullied because of the clothing they wore. Had they, along with all of the other students in the school, been made to wear uniforms that tragedy might have been averted.

If students were expected to wear uniforms, the cost of outfitting youth for school would be far less because there would be no need for "fashionable" wear.

THE RESOLUTION

Ms. Kolenek was not permitted to enforce her dress code. She remained with the school.

THIRTY-FOUR
Up the Down Stairs

In late February the principal of Olney Flowers High School drove off the road, overcorrected, and slammed into a truck in the opposite lane. His injuries were serious, and he would be unable to return to school for at least three months.

This led the school board to appoint Mr. Dale Essland interim principal. Mr. Essland had served as principal of Olney Flowers for eighteen years before his retirement sixteen years before. At the time of his interim appointment he had just celebrated his seventy-eighth birthday.

As it happened he took over as principal during a time of a major problem at Olney Flowers. Two months before, around Christmas time, the star running back on the football team from the previous fall, a junior named Medker Rivers, had been accused of sexual assault by a cheerleader named Tandy Gustovson. Rivers had not been arrested because Gustovson had not reported the incident until late January. There was little corroborating evidence and so it became a "he said," "she said" matter.

The problem was, as Mr. Essland soon discovered, that sides had been formed based on gender. A number of girls self-named Tandy's Troops held rallies demanding the arrest of Medker Rivers whose egotistic I'm-the-King-and-I-Can-Do-Whatever-I-Want personality offended them. A boys' group calling themselves Med's Friends, who feared that if Rivers were charged and convicted, they would lose their star for the next football season, came together as a counter to Tandy's Troops.

While not all of the Olney Flowers students joined either group, enough did to cause Mr. Essland real headaches. Med's Friends boys shouted down Tandy's Troops in hallway dustups.

The males had a favorite tactic of ascending the stairs to second floor classrooms directly behind Tandy's Troops girls and pinching their butts. The girls reciprocated by "gumming," whereby they picked out a member of Med's Friends, surrounded him, and in a synchronized motion took gum from their mouths and applied it their victim.

Of course, all manner of punishments were meted out to members of both groups: suspensions; in two cases (both boys of Med's Friends) expulsion; sweet reason with Mr. Essland and others of the faculty meeting with the student body. Parents became involved. They usually made matters worse. A security guard was hired. And yet the confrontations continued—in fact, became more bitter.

THE DILEMMA

Mr. Essland was at his wit's end. He wished devoutly he had never agreed to the interim appointment. The situation had become intolerable. Boys could not behave well around the girls; the girls could not behave well around the boys.

Mr. Essland harkened back to his high school days in a small school in southeastern Colorado. There, right from the get-go, the sexes were largely segregated. Boys took certain classes, e.g., basic aeronautics or woodshop. The girls took certain classes, e.g., home economics, shorthand.

And, Mr. Essland remembered, in his small high school there had been two sets of stairs. Only boys used the east stairs. Only girls used the west stairs. God help you if you were caught using the wrong side of stairs.

Because Onley Flowers had two main staircases, Mr. Essland mulled over the idea of instituting the stairs rule until the end of the semester. Moreover, he thought about reconfiguring classes in some way to have mostly one sex, if not all one sex, in a class.

Mr. Essland realized, of course, the rage his suggestion of one gender to a class would cause, particularly among those students not associated with either Tandy's Troops or Med's Friends. They would demand to know why they were being punished.

Yet he knew that many of the children's parents would support him. They recalled their high school days.

While Mr. Essland realized the "one class, one sex" idea was undoable that late in the semester, the stairs idea was not. An assigned stairway for each sex might help.

Maybe he should run his separate stairs idea past the school board members.

THE DEBATE

Pro

In the interests of defusing the standoff between Tandy's Troops and Med's Friends the separate stairs rule should be instituted and enforced. While that would not be easy to enforce nor would it stop all of the problems it would be a big help.

If it were possible to set up separate gender classes immediately, that would be a giant step forward, not only in putting an eventual end to the strife described, but in also facilitating learning.

Indeed, one of the biggest hurdles to effective education in America is the practice of having boys and girls in the same classes, especially from the sixth grade on through high school. The biggest reason that private and parochial school students score higher than public school students on standardized tests is because the former often do separate the sexes. In the interest of saving a bit of tax money (perhaps) and also in the interest of scheduling classes, public schools integrated the sexes at the expense of learning.

The reason that effective learning occurs more readily in the gender-separated schools should be abundantly evident to anyone. While the "males think about sex every seven seconds" myth has been thoroughly disproved, still—especially with regard to high school teens—for girls as well as boys, thoughts about the other sex cross their minds hundreds of times a day, thus quite obviously making it more difficult to focus on classroom learning while members of the opposite sex are present. Who doesn't know this?

Mr. Essland knows this. Indeed, every male and female with a normal sex drive knows this. If you put a pretty girl in the aisle next to a teenage boy, of course, his thoughts will wander to "boy, I'd like sex with her" instead of calculating the degrees of an acute angle.

But the same goes for the girl, too. If you put a handsome young man in the aisle next to her, she will be less able to remember the reasons for the Boston Tea Party.

Yes, Mr. Essland must be bold and propose his separate stairs idea. He should also argue for classes by gender arrangement for the following fall semester. It could be done, and it would improve learning in Olney Flowers High School significantly.

Con

Mr. Essland's idea of separate stairs is ridiculous. It might have worked toward hindering sexual thoughts and actions during the dark ages when Mr. Essland was a student, but today's young men and young women are far too "advanced" to obey such rules. Climbing one set of stairs or another will have utterly no effect on the students of Olney Flowers High School other than to cause resentment toward authority.

The notion of separating classes by gender is much more ridiculous. If this were attempted the students would *really* get angry.

Beyond the student anger there are other reasons for having boys and girls in the same classes (even home ec, woodshop, and auto mechanics). They are socializing; they are learning how to get along with each other. Students who are home schooled as well as many of those in private or parochial schools where they are sexually segregated often lack social skills, a very key requirement to function effectively in today's society.

The truth is that schools can really do nothing at all to damp down the normal sexual thoughts of young men and young women, and it is not the school's business to attempt to do so.

Mr. Essland does have a dilemma on his hands—how can Tandy's Troops and Med's Friends be controlled?—but his stairs idea will not do it.

THE RESOLUTION

Mr. Essland did put forth his boy stairs, girl stairs idea. None of the board members took it seriously. It was decided to suspend any student involved in Tandy Troop or Med's Friends activities for one week. A second involvement would cause the student to be expelled.

The situation at Olney Flowers gradually improved, and after the end of school in late May, Mr. Essland went back to his retirement.

THIRTY-FIVE
Here Come Better Grades

Delva Rolfson served as principal of Colonel Lynn High School, one of the four high schools in her city.

This Saturday night at eleven o'clock Ms. Rolfson sat in her office thinking about honesty and money.

Two years before, one Garvin Hessler, a man who had graduated from one of the city's high schools and had gone on to make millions in the high-tech field, had gifted large amounts of money to be distributed, some to each of the four high schools, but not in equal sums.

In an effort to improve student learning outcomes, Hessler's money was to be meted out on the basis of test score results, the tests having been developed by eight independent educators selected by Hessler himself.

The rules for determining the monies to be given to each high school were somewhat unusual. The tests would be given to only one hundred juniors in each high school, the students selected by a random drawing conducted by someone from outside the district. If the juniors taking the test achieved a seventy percent correct average score or higher, their school would receive one hundred thousand dollars. If the test takers in a second school achieved a similar result then that school would also receive one hundred thousand dollars. If the average of correct answers ranged between fifty and sixty-nine percent, then fifty thousand dollars would go to that school; if below fifty percent correct, only ten thousand dollars would go to that school.

THE DILEMMA

As she sat in her office that Saturday night Delva Rolfson wrestled with a question of conscience. The tests, which had been given on Saturday morning, were to have been handed over to a group of nine independent scorers upon the students completing them, but—big problem—a heavy snow storm had made it impossible for any of the scorers to reach the city.

The woman who had monitored the test takers had wanted to get back to her hotel before she had to stay at the school all night so she had consigned the one hundred completed tests to the safe at Delva's school with a warning to Delva that neither she nor anyone else should look at the tests.

Delva knew beyond all doubt that her students who had taken the test, all minority youth coming from the most impoverished area of the city, as a group would not have averaged better than fifty percent of their answers correct.

That afternoon, the woman monitor having left for her hotel, Delva who, of course, knew the combination to the safe where the tests were now stored awaiting the arrival of the scorers, sat at her desk considering the matter.

At length after everyone else had left the school around five o'clock, Delva succumbed to temptation. She opened the safe and removed the as-yet-ungraded tests. She picked twenty tests at random and looked at the answers. To her surprise, her juniors had performed better than she had expected, not above the fifty percent mark, she doubted, but close.

Now at eleven o'clock she looked at the notes she had scribbled to herself during the course of the evening and into the night. Among her notes, she had written these two sentences that stood out:

1. The big money will be going to the high school in the most affluent part of the district to help students who need the money much less than my students.
2. If my students received even the fifty thousand, we could and would improve our school significantly.

She knew that she could erase a few of the incorrect answers and substitute the right answers. Who would know? The students already showed a fair amount of erasures on their tests. She could stay most of the rest of the night and gain forty thousand dollars for her school.

She could then replace the tests in the safe. Who would know?

She considered the matter more. If she substituted the correct answers, her school would benefit and none of the other three schools would be given less money. So what was the harm?

If she were caught, she would be dismissed from her position and probably never would be able to hold a position in the field of education again.

She slid a test sheet onto her desk in front of her, turned a pencil eraser down, and . . . paused.

Should she erase?

THE DEBATE

Pro

Delva should erase. The terms of Hessler's gift are opposite of what they should be. If his intention is to improve education in the four schools in the district, he should restructure the rules. Either he should give each school the same amount of money and not use tests at all, or he should give a lesser amount to the school in the most affluent part of the city and a greater amount to Delva's school. He should not use the tests his people have designed (which probably have low validity for Delva's students anyway). Rather he should use tax figures that show the degree of wealth in the separate parts of the city and base his giving on those figures.

Does Delva run some risk to herself and her career in changing the test answers? Yes, of course she does, however, she should do it because (1) her chances of being caught for changing the test answers are low; (2) the money will help her school and its students significantly; and (3) she will only be righting what is the wrong way to distribute the money anyway.

So go for it, Delva. Do what is right!

Con

Delva, what if you would find that one of your students had cheated to gain an undeserved advantage over another of your students? You would punish the cheater, would you not?

That is really all, Delva. Enough said.

However, there is a good and substantial reason why Mr. Hessler designed his gifting in the manner he has. I will start with an analogy: let us say a track coach has two athletes, one an exceptionally good hurdler, nearly world class but not quite, and the other a distance runner who is mediocre at best. Now where should the coach spend the greater amount of his time coaching?

The answer is obvious. He should spend his time with the hurdler to assist him to get to the world-class level. The distance runner is never going to get significantly better. Help him a bit, but don't spend much time with him.

The same obvious conclusion applies here. The students with the higher test average in all probability will contribute much more to the world than the students with the lower average. It is simply a matter of intelligence.

Mr. Hessler understands this.

No, Delva, do not change the test scores.

Chapter 35

THE RESOLUTION

Delva Rolfson put the eraser on an answer. She paused. She gathered the tests and returned them to the safe. She locked the front door of Colonel Lynn High School and walked home in the snow, arriving at her house at two in the morning.

She decided on Sunday that she would write a letter to Mr. Garvin Hessler thanking him for his gift to her school, but also explaining why his system was wrong.

THIRTY-SIX
Precious

Fred Anders taught American history in a northern California high school. One morning as the students were reading silently, a mousey little girl named Precious came to his desk to ask a question about the Liberty Bell pictured on the front of her textbook. "How come it's broke?" she asked.

Fred knew there were several versions of how the Liberty Bell came to be cracked, but rather than confuse Precious, his poorest student, he chose to give her only one story. He interrupted the other members of the class and said, "Precious has asked a great question. You all need to hear the question and the answer to it."

Precious repeated the question for all the class to hear. "How come the bell's broke?"

Fred gave the answer. "In 1835, tolling for the funeral of Chief Justice John Marshall, the bell cracked and was never repaired."

A few days later he gave a quiz. One of the questions was: "Why is the Liberty Bell cracked?" He was sure Precious would answer that question correctly.

Precious handed in her paper. Fred read her answer: "They was being chased by the marshal of justice, and when they got to the toll booth they dropped it and it broke."

THE DILEMMA

Fred wondered what grade he should give Precious. She had completely mangled the answer. Yet, on the other hand, she had been the student who had asked the original question. She had been interested at least.

THE DEBATE

Pro

Precious had asked the question. Pass her.

Con

Too bad, but Precious must receive a failing grade. She has grasped nothing from the answer Fred gave.

THE RESOLUTION

Several months later on the last day of school as Fred was putting all of the textbooks in the closet of his room there came a light knock on his classroom door. He opened the door. There stood Precious and two other girls, her friends. Precious asked, "Can we come in?"

"Sure, come on in."

Precious cleared her throat and said, "We heard you're leavin', Mr. Anders."

"Yes, that's right. I'm going back to Iowa to teach at a college."

"We're sorry."

"What?" asked Mr. Anders.

"I said we're sorry."

"Why are you sorry, Precious?"

"Because we love you, Teach."

Mr. Anders knew right then he had made the right decision in giving Precious a passing grade.

And he knew right then, too, why he had entered the teaching profession.

The End

About the Author

Richard Kimbrough, an educator for fifty-seven years in classrooms from middle school through graduate studies, has taught in schools from California to Illinois to Central Asia. For thirty-five years, he has spoken annually to between fifty to seventy-five educational groups relating to common classroom problems and their solutions.

www.ingramcontent.com/pod-product-compliance
Lightning Source LLC
Chambersburg PA
CBHW030141240426
43672CB00005B/218